The Inspired Hybrid Classroom

Kimberly Merritt, Elizabeth P. Callaghan,
Stephen M. Kosslyn, Editors

ALINEA

Alinea Learning
Boston

ALINEA

Alinea Learning

Boston, Massachusetts

Published in the United States by Alinea Learning, an imprint and division of Alinea Knowledge, LLC, Boston.

Copyright © 2025 by Alinea Knowledge, LLC

All rights reserved. No part of this book may be reproduced in any manner without the express written consent of Alinea Learning. Reprint requests should be addressed to info@alinealearning.com.

Visit our website at www.alinealearning.com.

Library of Congress Cataloging-in-Publication Data is available on file.

Print book ISBN: 979-8-9878531-9-1

eBook ISBN: 979-8-9878531-2-2

Cover design by Imprudent Press, LLC

Cover Copyright © 2025 by Alinea Knowledge, LLC

Table of Contents

Introduction 7
    What is the New Hybrid?
        Kimberly Merritt, Elizabeth P. Callaghan, Stephen M. Kosslyn

PART 1 11
    Why to Hybrid
        Kimberly Merritt, Elizabeth P. Callaghan, Stephen M. Kosslyn
    Chapter 1 13
        Kimberly Merritt
        Why to Hybrid: A Holistic Look at the Challenges that Face our Current Educational Systems and the Benefits of Designing Hybrid College Models
    Chapter 2 29
        Stephen M. Kosslyn
        Many Types of Hybrid Courses are the Future of Education
    Chapter 3 59
        Maria Anguiano
        The Equity Imperative: Putting Learners' Needs at the Heart of Higher Education Design

PART 2 77
    How to Hybrid
        Kimberly Merritt, Elizabeth P. Callaghan, Stephen M. Kosslyn
    Chapter 4 79
        John Katzman and Melora Sundt
        An Agile University Structure for Hybrid Course Design
    Chapter 5 93
        David P. Green
        Ensuring Success when Developing Hybrid Learning Interventions
    Chapter 6 111
        Aaron Rasmussen and Kristen Przyborski
        Subdividing Synchrony: Finding Opportunities for Meaningful Interaction in Online Courses
    Chapter 7 125
        Elizabeth P. Callaghan
        Effective Learning Objectives in the Hybrid Classroom

Chapter 8 139
    Shaunak Roy and Brian Verdine
    Hybrid Learning Across Time and Space

PART 3 .... **169**
    Use Cases of Hybrid
        Kimberly Merritt, Elizabeth P. Callaghan, Stephen M. Kosslyn
    Chapter 9 171
        Duane Roen
        Using the "Available Means": Learning to ~~Write~~ Compose in A New American University
    Chapter 10 185
        Maria Anguiano and Kimberly Merritt
        ASU Local: A Case Study of a Community-Based Hybrid College Model
    Chapter 11 203
        Kellie Kreiser
        DreamBuilder: A Study in Developing and Modifying Hybrid Training Over Time
    Chapter 12 233
        Meredyth Hendricks & Stuart Rice
        Catalyzing Careers with Hybrid Learning

Afterword **265**
    The AI Revolution in Hybrid College Education
        Kimberly Merritt, Elizabeth P. Callaghan, Stephen M. Kosslyn

Introduction

What is the New Hybrid?

Kimberly Merritt, Elizabeth P. Callaghan, Stephen M. Kosslyn

Education has undergone a radical transformation in recent years, with the rise of online learning, digital technologies and new pedagogical approaches. The year 2020 marked a tipping point as the COVID-19 pandemic forced a rapid shift to remote learning, creating an unprecedented demand for innovative and effective teaching and learning methods. In the aftermath of the pandemic, educators are increasingly exploring the potential of hybrid learning, which combines online and in-person components to create a more flexible, accessible, and engaging educational experience.

Hybrid education combines elements of both traditional in-person teaching and online teaching and can be either synchronous (live) or asynchronous (not live). It aims to take advantage of the benefits of different modes of instruction to create a learning experience that is engaging, flexible, and effective. Depending on how modalities are combined (virtual, in-person, synchronous, or asynchronous), each learning experience can be tailored to meet the needs of specific populations and educational goals.

The move to hybrid education was originally largely driven by the COVID-19 pandemic, which made it necessary for many schools and universities to transition to online teaching. However, many educators and students have found that online teaching has its own unique advantages, such as increased flexibility and the ability to support more active and engaging learning. As a result, many schools and universities are now exploring the potential of hybrid education as a way to take advantage of the benefits of different teaching modalities.

The Inspired Hybrid Classroom is a guide to this new and rapidly evolving field, providing insight and guidance to instructors at all levels of education who are seeking to harness the power of hybrid learning. Drawing on Arizona State University's and its affiliates' expertise, this book explores the different forms of hybrid education, the lessons learned from specific cases, the applicability to different populations, and the projections for future developments. The book is divided into three sections: the first section reviews foundational concepts, the second covers methods and best practices, and the third summarizes specific case studies.

The chapters in this book, written by experts from academia and industry, bridge the gap between theory and practice, exploring a wide range of topics, including the design of hybrid learning experiences, the different types of hybrid courses, the role of hybrid education in promoting equity, the role of hybrid learning in career development, the importance of an agile university structure, and many more. With its engaging and practical approach, *The Inspired Hybrid Classroom* provides an essential resource for anyone seeking to understand and utilize the full potential of hybrid learning.

Chapters 1-3 serve as a broad overview of the new hybrid model: what it is and why we need it. These chapters provide content on the philosophical underpinnings of why and how hybrid classes can be used to revolutionize how learning can be delivered. **Chapters 4-8** outline best practices and institutional structures that facilitate hybrid learning. Finally, **Chapters 9-12** represent hybrid in action: use cases that illustrate the power and benefits of hybrid education. They do a deep dive into various use cases and detailed observations from practitioners and designers in the field. The book presents voices from technology creators to classroom implementers and provides insight into how to create active, thoughtful hybrid learning design.

Chapter 1 focuses on the ways that educators can design a student experience that meets learning goals and helps students thrive in the hybrid learning environment. The goal of the hybrid experience is to balance the best aspects of online and in-person instruction to create accessible and engaging learning design.

Chapter 2 explores the different types of hybrid courses, including the differences between synchronous and asynchronous modes and the different combinations of online and in-person settings. The chapter outlines the advantages of each type of hybrid course depending on the specific course goals, constraints, and resources.

Chapter 3 discusses the challenges students face in the current college system, which was not designed with their needs in mind. It argues that higher education opportunities should be structured to put learners' needs and dreams at the heart of every design decision—and that hybrid designs can promote this goal.

Chapter 4 begins the second section and argues that hybrid courses require an agile university infrastructure to support, recruit, and place students and professors, regardless of the particular teaching modality they choose.

Chapter 5 provides a conceptual model for improving organizational support in hybrid environments. It outlines ways to align with instructors' social and creative identities, which should be useful for trainers and educators guiding educational reform initiatives.

Chapter 6 focuses on how to use a hybrid model to make the most of synchronous teaching, which is the most valuable and scarce resource in education. It provides an overview of best practices for selecting the most appropriate modality for each aspect of a course, such as instructor-synchronous, peer-synchronous one-to-one, peer-synchronous one-to-many, AI-synchronous, and asynchronous.

Chapter 7 discusses the use of learning objectives in hybrid courses, which can often be haphazard and disconnected at the individual class level. It outlines the benefits of using granular learning objectives for each class session to guide learning and connect asynchronous activities to those in the classroom.

Chapter 8 explores the challenge of blending online/asynchronous learning with in-person/synchronous learning to create a cohesive educational experience. The chapter discusses high-impact pedagogical practices, technology choices, and design principles to help bridge the gap and make the learning experience more seamless.

Chapter 9 begins the final section of the book and describes a case study of the rise and evolution of hybrid learning at Arizona State University, with a focus on writing instruction. The chapter covers the innovations in hybrid writing instruction from the late 1990s to the present and reflects on future experiences that could support hybrid lifelong learning.

Chapter 10 examines the development and modification of an online women's entrepreneurship program as a case study for creating and adapting a hybrid training program. The chapter explores the impact of changes in technology and participant abilities on the program and how different modalities can preserve its effectiveness.

Chapter 11 illustrates how hybrid learning can be used to bring a community together to support youth and increase college persistence and life outcomes. It also addresses the lessons learned from the program.

Chapter 12 examines the impact of automation on the workforce, which is estimated to threaten 47% of jobs. It argues that lifelong learning will be essential for workers to keep their skills up to date. The chapter explores the benefits of hybrid learning for career-long employee learning, engagement, and team culture and examines the key components of a skills-oriented hybrid learning program in a corporate setting.

PART 1

Why to Hybrid

Kimberly Merritt, Elizabeth P. Callaghan, Stephen M. Kosslyn

Part Introduction: Embracing the Future of Education

The Inspired Hybrid Classroom is a comprehensive exploration of the transformative potential of hybrid approaches to teaching and learning. In this first section, we focus on the compelling reasons to embrace hybrid education and the benefits it offers to students, educators, and society at large. We delve into the unique advantages of hybrid education, its myriad forms, use cases, and the opportunities it provides for evolving education to better serve diverse populations and address 21st-century challenges.

Over the course of the chapters in this section, we review many ways that hybrid education can enhance the learning experience, foster inclusivity, and prepare students for the rapidly changing world. At its core, the hybrid model seeks to reimagine the college experience so that it's more accessible to a wider population of students; it does so by adjusting pedagogy and program design to improve learning outcomes for all. Hybrid education has the power to break down barriers and expand access to quality education for students from diverse backgrounds. Moreover, an evolution to hybrid education creates opportunities for new financial paradigms in the prioritization of programs.

The concepts and methods in this section outline the ways that hybrid education can be used to solve many challenges in higher education. With an expanding population and fewer resources, hybrid modalities can be used to personalize the learning experience and support instructors in a system with ever-growing demands on their time. And using hybrid modalities can enhance collaboration and communication among both faculty and students. As the workplace becomes more hybrid itself, mirroring that shift in education prepares students for rapidly changing 21st-century employment.

We invite you to join us on this journey to explore how this innovative approach can shape the future of teaching and learning for the better.

Chapter 1

Kimberly Merritt

Why to Hybrid: A Holistic Look at the Challenges that Face our Current Educational Systems and the Benefits of Designing Hybrid College Models

Abstract

This chapter delves into the significance of hybrid education, a blend of online and in-person instruction, in fostering accessible and engaging learning experiences for an increasingly diverse learner population. Hybrid education, when well-executed, offers flexibility, career alignment, and personalization to meet individual learners' needs. It is crucial to address biases and actively engage with student feedback to implement hybrid programming successfully. The COVID-19 pandemic has accentuated the need for hybrid learning, but its importance extends beyond emergency measures. By re-evaluating the core tenets of higher education design, we can better understand our learners and address the gaps in serving diverse demographics. The chapter calls for a critical assessment of higher education's success and the potential of hybrid learning to revolutionize the future of education.

This chapter describes the benefits of effectively crafting hybrid student experiences that promote deeper learning and enable an ever-growing learner population to gain access to high-quality educational experiences. The goal of hybrid schools and courses is to strike a balance between online and in-person instruction, thereby creating accessible and engaging learning design. When executed well, hybrid education has the potential to revolutionize the future of education by offering flexibility, career alignment, and personalized approaches tailored to individual learners' needs.

To truly serve contemporary learners, including those who are first-generation or experiencing poverty, we must be open to hybrid programming and avoid biases that can cloud discussions. This requires active engagement with students' feedback and a willingness to challenge long-held assumptions.

Leaders must have the courage to ask difficult questions and receive honest answers about what is and is not working in the higher education system.

The Challenges Facing Current Education Systems
Need for Hybrid

Online degrees and hybrid learning certainly existed pre-pandemic, but the onset of the COVID-19 pandemic in 2020 catapulted online education and hybrid learning to the center of higher education conversation. Yet the need for hybrid learning existed long before the pandemic and remains post-pandemic as well. The need goes beyond emergency measures and calls us to revisit the core tenets of higher education design. We need to consider why individuals choose to pursue a college degree and who our "customers" are. We need to understand how successful we have been in the support of our learners and honestly wrestle through why we may not have been as successful as we would have hoped for all demographics. It is in the context of those fundamental questions, or higher ed soul searching that the need for hybrid learning becomes clear.

Deconstructing the Purpose of College for the Majority of Learners

The aspiration to complete college is almost universally shared by learners. Although the holistic benefits of college are many, approximately 74% of learners seek a college degree to gain upward mobility via enhanced career opportunities (Lumina Foundation, 2016). For many learners and families, choosing higher education (and the resulting debt) goes beyond having the college experience depicted in the movies or pursuing a passion. For many, it is the promise of a better life. Parents of first-generation students may have worked their entire lives to provide such an opportunity to their children, believing that it would open doors for their families that would remain otherwise shut.

A college degree has become an important step in the pursuit of the American dream and a gatekeeper of sorts on the path from generational poverty to generational wealth. According to the US Bureau of Labor Statistics, the median weekly earnings for an individual with a bachelor's degree is $1,334 compared to that of a high school graduate at $809 (BLS, 2021).

The Current System Is Not Meeting Learners or Communities Needs

Despite increased numbers of students attending college and hoping to earn college degrees, entire subsets of the student population are being left behind (Basch et al., 2015), and, unfortunately, colleges infrequently reassess their role in ensuring that students see and attain the two core values in attaining a college degree: reaching a college degree goal and getting a great job.

Students often grow up with the vision of college degree attainment as a shining accomplishment on their lifelong journey. This is reinforced throughout their K-12 experience and often within their family narratives (Souto-Manning, 2017; Stephens et al., 2014). In this American narrative, the path to success and upward mobility is a college degree (Laird & Kienzl, 2017; Baum et al., 2013). We must ask whether this narrative or ideal is attainable or even possible for the diversity of our citizens with the current systems we have designed. Given this narrative of success, what happens when the colleges we have designed don't meet the realities of the lives our college hopefuls live? College persistence rates for students experiencing poverty are disproportionately low, suggesting there is a disconnect between these students' desires and the realities of our current college system (Soria et al., 2014; Pascarella & Terenzini, 2005).

Merely accessing postsecondary education alone is a labyrinthine challenge. Students must have developed college aspirations, understand the college application and enrollment processes, have the financial ability to pay college tuition, and engage in a college system that meets their needs. However, navigating these college steps described above is a complex process that is often difficult, particularly for those who do not have the benefit of family members who have previously navigated the maze. This process further distances the reality of the current college system from learners' needs. The dream of college degree attainment is rife with examples such as this, where despite a deep desire to succeed, learners do not graduate from college.

Although the goal of learning for the sake of learning is core to who we are as humans, learners also want to use college degrees to access better jobs, and the American economy wants college graduates. Demand for college-educated workers is growing. College degrees provide students access to diverse careers and the middle class (Hongwei, 2015) and ensure that the American economy has a skilled workforce to meet demand. In theory, a college education is a much-needed vehicle for upward mobility that gives all demographics access to these much-needed jobs to fuel the American economy. Yet, the reality is a starker picture. Learners rarely have a true concept of or applied skills in the workforce they seek to enter post-degree. They rack-up massive amounts of debt —often without a career trajectory to match the debt level. Most importantly, the system isn't designed for their needs, and they often leave college with unrecognizable college credits not fit for a resume and without the promised prize of a degree to leverage as they enter the workforce.

The goal of gaining a degree and getting a great job is almost universal for today's college students, but higher ed leaders have yet to embrace a learner-first design to support learners in meeting these goals (Jorgenson & Ahlburg, 2015). The current college system, as designed, does not account for the unique needs of learners, and historically, colleges suggested that the reason for this failure has been the student's deficiencies. It would not be out of character for schools to ask " why can't they do this' ' when discussing students challenged in the system. Colleges then create well-intentioned solutions based on questions like "How do we better prepare students to succeed in our college system?" The real question—we posit—is, "How do we listen to learners?" How do we understand what learners need, and then how do we change our system to meet those needs? The American education system is poised to undergo a dramatic shift to address persistent gaps in historically disadvantaged students' success. Our current education model is not designed to address these glaring gaps, thus creating a need for new hybrid systems that can be designed with learners' needs at the forefront of programmatic design (Basch et al., 2015; Hongwei, 2015).

Deconstructing the traditional college framework ("how college works")

We in higher ed are involved in a noble mission. We know that a college degree is a key to social mobility and generational wealth. While we understand this mission and seek the success of our learners, it is also true that higher ed is slow to change. We are often reluctant to have difficult conversations about why students may not be finding success in our systems and even more reluctant to make systematic changes. Often "the way we have always done it" wins the day. But as society changes and our demographics change, that reluctance and those "sacred cows" inhibit the further success of our learners.

In higher ed, we tend to be adders. We like additive solutions. We like to add elements to current programs or to add entire brand-new programs. We tack-on solutions and see the value of expansion. In this book, we propose that it is important for us to move in the other direction. It is time for us to deconstruct: time to deconstruct our courses, our degree offerings, our support systems, our delivery modalities. We are not suggesting that we dismantle our systems outright, but to deconstruct them in such a way that we bring a critical, analytical lens to see whether our current systems still meet their original intent and whether they are maximizing the success of our learners. After all, shouldn't we be involved in that type of analytical rigor? Truly advancing equity will require this deconstruction so that we no longer merely tack on those additive structures with minimal success but actually correct historical design flaws or emerging design flaws and re-design with equity and student success at the forefront.

Asking the questions posed above and deconstructing our courses and degrees will inevitably lead to a conversation about hybrid programming and will challenge us to explore the potential benefits of the online components to our programs and maximizing how we spend our time in person. Maybe we will find that the benefits go beyond equity and flexibility. Maybe there are sound pedagogical reasons for online components and an envisioning of in-person work that makes up higher education. Maybe deepening our view of learning and providing flexibility will make our degrees more powerful and practical for the needs of today's world. As we dig into the make-up of degrees, we also invite you to take a critical look at the what, the why and the how that is embedded in the challenge of educating the over seven billion people in the world. What does a degree entail; Why are each of the components necessary for a modern education; How do we prepare to educate the over seven billion people in the world?

A Note on the Pandemic

Although the pandemic opened the door to hybrid learning across the country, for many in higher ed with little prior experience, it also colored perceptions of what hybrid learning is, what it looks like, and, more importantly, what it *feels* like. If first impressions affect our long-term perceptions, then for many, their ongoing relation to hybrid might be skewed. Additionally, most students' first exposure to hybrid occurred during a time of immense fear and confusion in the world more broadly.

Institutions made the pivot to hybrid learning under challenging circumstances, but often this change simply entailed moving a fully in-person course completely online, then when in-person became possible again, schools instituted a mixture of online learning with haphazard in-person options. There was no time to redesign for the new modality or to maximize the benefits of hybrid learning. While these decisions were necessitated by circumstance, they may have resulted in a distorted understanding of what hybrid learning is. One of our goals in this book is to correct the record, to illustrate the rich benefits of hybrid learning, and to demonstrate what it can look like when done well. As we flow through this chapter and this book, it will be important to remember that what we created as a response to the pandemic does not represent the true potential of hybrid learning.

Benefits of Hybrid

As the student population diversifies and the needs of modern learners differ from those of previous generations, institutions must adapt to serve all students effectively. Hybrid learning offers a flexible model that meets the needs of a range of learners, from those requiring a more flexible schedule to those seeking a more personalized approach. By embracing hybrid instruction, institutions can also increase their adaptability and better prepare themselves for future crises, as well as attract new students at a lower cost structure. Partnerships with outside industries and organizations provide additional opportunities for innovation and collaboration, benefiting both students and institutions alike. Finally, hybrid learning aligns with contemporary changes in employment modalities, preparing learners for the hybrid work options that are increasingly available in the job market. This section emphasizes the importance of hybrid learning as a means of creating a more equitable, adaptable, and effective higher education system, with a particular emphasis on equity, agility, cost structure, partnerships, and 21st-century programming benefits.

Equity

Proponents of online and hybrid learning always knew that there was a segment of prospective students that would benefit from a more flexible model than the traditional 100% in-person instruction model prevalent in higher ed. What is quickly coming into sharper focus is just how many of our modern learners would not merely benefit from this flexible model but need it. In later chapters, we draw a profile of a modern learner and describe how her needs from a higher ed institution likely differ from that of a traditional student. Depending on the learners, those needs might differ drastically.

Institutions must wrestle with the future of hybrid learning. Is there space in the new normal to expand hybrid learning, or will an institution revert to a predominantly in-person model? We propose that this question goes beyond a juxtaposition of learning modalities. It is a question of who we are serving and how we enable their success. At its heart, it is a question of equity.

As college demographics change, not just in terms of race but also socioeconomics, the needs of the modern student will also look quite different from previous generations. Students experiencing poverty often lack the support needed to access and graduate from college, thereby creating a gap in the level of success achieved by different sub-groups of students (Baugh et al., 2019; Joy, 2017). Current educational structures have yet to efficiently address this gap and create effective systems that meet the needs of these historically underrepresented students. This conclusion is supported by evidence demonstrating low college graduation rates for college- and university-qualified historically disadvantaged students (Dahill-Brown et al., 2016). Historically disadvantaged students have faced systematic limitations in their access to and success in college when compared to other student populations. Thus, these groups are often excluded from middle- and upper-class jobs and wages. These individuals are more likely to live in low-income areas and are often unable to access resources that can lead to prosperity (Caspar, 2015; Muskens et al., 2019). The need to work full time, navigate family responsibilities, and complete remedial coursework requirements have all affected timely college enrollment and often lead to part-time enrollment and a longer time to degree attainment (Falcon, 2020).

As enrollment of first-generation learners, underrepresented populations, and those who experience poverty increases, institutions must also consider how best to enable their success and how the broader context of their lives impacts their education. We assert that the foundation of the conversation, the need and drive for hybrid learning, is a moral mandate to purposefully include and equally serve those who do not fit the historical college student archetype. Often practices such as lecture-based learning, standardized testing, traditional grading systems, limited interdisciplinary collaboration, semester-based academic calendar, high tuition costs, and over-reliance on a central physical campus are often unchallenged. The changing landscape will require bold leadership and difficult conversations to determine whether current institutional structures are able to meet the needs of the time.

Agility

Expanding hybrid instruction not only enhances the learning experience but also boosts the adaptability of institutions. College campuses with little to no existing hybrid instruction faced significant challenges when the pandemic hit, resulting in varied experiences for both students and faculty across different institutions and departments.

However, by embracing hybrid instruction and incorporating it into the higher education system, institutions can better prepare themselves for future crises. Whether it's a pandemic, natural disaster, or some other emergency, institutions with a hybrid structure in place will be better equipped to navigate uncertain circumstances. In today's fast-paced world, adaptability is essential, and hybrid instruction is a valuable tool for institutions looking to stay ahead of the curve.

Cost Structure

Hybrid instruction also helps to address a key concern of prospective students and parents: prohibitive costs. As the country grapples with the rising costs of a degree and many wonder how and when they will see a return on investment, the value proposition of higher education is being questioned more explicitly today than it has in previous decades. With enrollments trending down across the country, higher education institutions must figure out ways to move forward with fewer tuition dollars and, for public institutions, often fewer state dollars as well. Because traditional courses typically depend on in-person instruction, there is a high corresponding capital infrastructure cost for the institution. Adding students often then means adding additional capital infrastructure. There will still be infrastructure needs in hybrid learning, but the amount and type will be vastly different than traditional instruction and may result in a lower cost structure. Those savings may be passed along to students or provide for additional investments in key areas such as student success. Hybrid learning allows an institution to maximize its current capital resources and attract new students at a lower cost structure.

Partnerships

Hybrid learning structures offer a revolutionary approach to education, unlocking the potential to tap into partnerships, both local and global, and forge a new vision of what learning can be. By collaborating with outside organizations and industry leaders, higher education institutions can harness diverse skills, talents, and innovations beyond their walls. This is particularly vital in the realm of hybrid learning, where unconventional schedules and learning designs can help students tap into local expertise earlier in their academic journey—an opportunity that was once reserved for post-graduation. However, traditional learning frameworks often hinder the formation of meaningful local partnerships, despite their potential to enhance the learning experience.

Accessing partnerships can be challenging within the constraints of traditional higher education frameworks. This is because traditional models of higher education prioritize maintaining a closed system of education, with a strong emphasis on theoretical learning, research, and publication. As a result, institutions may find it challenging to connect with local organizations and industry leaders due to a lack of resources or a limited focus on community engagement. Additionally, universities may also face bureaucratic hurdles, such as navigating institutional policies and regulations, which can impede their ability to form meaningful partnerships with external organizations. In contrast, hybrid learning structures, with their more flexible and adaptive approaches, can provide an alternative means of overcoming these barriers and forging valuable connections with the local community.

Theoretical barriers aside, the traditional education construct of seat time—often literally taken to mean time learning while in a seat—does not lend itself to honoring learning that is place-based and applied. A hybrid model allows us to continue to meet the construct of seat time but frees students up to attend partnership location settings in the 9-5 structure many high-paying, upwardly mobile jobs have.

In the context of hybrid learning, local partnerships prove to be particularly valuable because they provide tailored education that meets the unique needs and interests of the local community. For instance, a partnership with a local tech company can provide students with practical exposure to relevant technologies and prepare them for promising careers in the tech industry. Meanwhile, collaborating with community organizations can open doors to internships, networking events, and other resources that support academic and professional growth. Ultimately, students stand to gain the most from these partnerships, as they can access a broader range of opportunities and resources that go beyond what the institution can offer alone.

21st Century Programming

Hybrid learning is also well aligned with changes in work modalities. With increasing numbers of employers offering hybrid work options for employees, the skills learners develop in a hybrid environment prepare them for not only *what* they will be doing in their jobs but *how* they will be doing it. Hybrid learning offers learners a unique opportunity to develop skills that are essential for success in the 21st-century workforce. In today's fast-paced, constantly changing work environments, employees need to be adaptable and flexible, often needing to be able to work effectively both in-person and remotely. Hybrid learning prepares learners for this type of work by teaching them how to balance their time, prioritize tasks, and manage their workload, no matter where they are located.

When collaborative experiences are prioritized in the hybrid setting, it also promotes an environment of collaboration and communication, skills that are highly valued by employers. In virtual settings, effective communication is key, and hybrid learning provides learners with ample opportunities to hone their ability to work effectively in online teams. By engaging in group projects, online discussions, and in-person and virtual presentations, learners can develop the skills they need to communicate their ideas effectively, work collaboratively towards common goals, and thrive in fast-paced, dynamic work environments—all in multiple modern modalities.

My dad often commented that nothing teaches someone to get good at something faster than doing it, and my first day as a teacher confirmed it for me. This adage supports leveraging hybrid learning to ensure the powerful theoretical and humanistic education, paired with applied learning can ignite new neurological connections and deepen learning. The embedded practice in switching modalities can help learners maximize technology usage and become proficient in 21st-century workforce strategies like using virtual collaboration tools and online project management platforms. Broadly, as learners practice skill attainment and deliverable completion in college much in the same manner they will be doing it in the workforce, they are likely to enter the workforce much better prepared to be of value immediately.

Conclusions

This chapter discussed the potential of hybrid learning, the misconceptions resulting from its rapid adoption during the pandemic, and its benefits in today's evolving educational landscape. Hybrid learning offers a flexible model that meets the diverse needs of modern learners, allowing institutions to serve a broader range of students and promote equity. This book highlights five key benefits: equity, agility, cost structure, partnerships, and 21st-century programming. Emphasizing the importance of adaptability, hybrid learning prepares institutions for future crises and helps reduce costs, making education more accessible. By fostering local partnerships, hybrid learning encourages collaboration and innovation, while 21st-century programming aligns with current workforce trends, equipping students with the skills needed to succeed in the modern, hybrid work environment.

In later chapters, we will delve deeper into the mechanics of hybrid learning. Hybrid learning encompasses various combinations of in-person and online education and is not a one-size-fits-all approach. We will provide definitions and examples of different hybrid learning permutations, demonstrating the vast possibilities available in this framework. The goal is to encourage educators and institutions to expand their horizons, listen to their learners, and design with the full flexibility and creativity that hybrid learning allows. These practical guides serve as a valuable resource for those eager to explore and implement hybrid learning models in their own educational environments and as a springboard into the hybrid case studies that follow.

References

Baum, S., Ma, J., & Payea, K. (2013). Education Pays 2013: The Benefits of Higher Education for Individuals and Society. The College Board.

Basch, C. E., Basch, C. H., Ruggles, K. V., & Rajan, S. (2015). Prevalence of sleep duration on an average school night among 4 nationally representative successive samples of American high school students, 2007–2013. Preventive Medicine, 73, 52-53.

Bureau of Labor Statistics. (2021). Earnings and unemployment rates by educational attainment. US Department of Labor. Retrieved from https://www.bls.gov/emp/chart-unemployment-earnings-education.htm

Hongwei, Z. (2015). The effect of college education on three domains of quality of life: A longitudinal study in the United States. Social Indicators Research, 120(3), 851-867.

Jorgenson, S., & Ahlburg, D. (2015). Redesigning the MBA: A Curriculum Development Study. Journal of Education for Business, 90(1), 9-15.

Laird, T. F., & Kienzl, G. S. (2017). The 2016 National Survey of Student Engagement (NSSE) Annual Results. Indiana University Center for Postsecondary Research.

Lumina Foundation. (2016). A Stronger Nation: Postsecondary Learning Builds the Talent That Helps Us Rise. Lumina Foundation.

Pascarella, E. T., & Terenzini, P. T. (2005). How college affects students: A third decade of research. Jossey-Bass.

Soria, K. M., Weiner, B., & Lu, E. C. (2014). Financial decisions among undergraduate students from low-income and working-class social backgrounds. Journal of Student Financial Aid, 44(1), 2.

Souto-Manning, M. (2017). Early childhood education as a "white" space: Re-centering social justice in education. International Journal of Early Childhood, 49(1), 109-124.

Stephens, N. M., Hamedani, M. G., & Destin, M. (2014). Closing the social-class achievement gap: A difference-education intervention improves first-generation students' academic performance and all students' college transition. Psychological Science, 25(4), 943-953.

Baugh, S. G., Graff, C., Hudak, S. L., & Keeley, M. E. (2019). First-generation college students and academic libraries: A systematic literature review. College & Research Libraries, 80(6), 752-770.

Caspar, A. (2015). Socioeconomic status and access to higher education: A quantitative analysis of factors that hinder college enrollment. Journal of College Admission, 228, 30-37.

Dahill-Brown, S. E., Lavery, L., & Meyers, C. V. (2016). Is education policy "normal" now? Resources, standards, and courts in the US states. Publius: The Journal of Federalism, 46(1), 1-25.

Falcon, L. (2020). Supporting the academic success of Hispanic students. Education Digest, 85(5), 23-28.

Joy, G. (2017). Closing the gap: Identifying factors that contribute to low college enrollment rates among first-generation, low-income, and minority students. Journal of College Admission, 234, 26-35.

Muskens, G., Brinkkemper, S., & Blom, M. (2019). Bridging the gap: Socioeconomic status, social capital, and higher education enrollment. Education and Urban Society, 51(7), 961-984.

Cedefop. (2020). The digitalisation of work: Implications for skills and employment. European Centre for the Development of Vocational Training. Retrieved from https://www.cedefop.europa.eu/en/publications-and-resources/publications/9129

Hart Research Associates. (2015). Falling short? College learning and career success. Association of American Colleges and Universities. Retrieved from https://www.aacu.org/sites/default/files/files/LEAP/2015employerstudentsurvey.pdf

Means, B., Bakia, M., & Murphy, R. (2014). Learning online: What research tells us about whether, when, and how. Routledge.

Pellegrino, J. W., & Hilton, M. L. (2012). Education for life and work: Developing transferable knowledge and skills in the 21st century. National Academies Press.

Seaman, J. E., Allen, I. E., & Seaman, J. (2018). Grade increase: Tracking distance education in the United States. Babson Survey Research Group. Retrieved from https://onlinelearningsurvey.com/reports/gradeincrease.pdf

Chapter 2

Stephen M. Kosslyn

Many Types of Hybrid Courses are the Future of Education

Abstract

Hybrid classes are created by combining different teaching modalities. This chapter distinguishes among different types of hybrid designs by considering ways to combine four different teaching modalities. These modalities emerge from a simple 2 x 2 table, where the columns are defined by Synchronous versus Asynchronous modes, and the rows are defined by Online versus In-Person settings. The appropriate uses of different combinations of the resulting four teaching modalities are described in the context of the course designer's goals, constraints, and available resources.

The Covid pandemic forced many instructors to teach their courses online, and many believed that both faculty and students would abandon online courses as soon as they possibly could. For instance, on June 5th, 2020, the *Wall Street Journal* published an article entitled "The results are in for remote learning: It didn't work" (Hobbs & Hawkins, 2020). As it turned out, this verdict was premature. In fact, as the pandemic continued to force instructors to teach online, they not only adapted but also realized that teaching remotely had some advantages over traditional in-person teaching (e.g., DeWitt, 2021; Singer, 2021). For example, teaching online affords greater flexibility in scheduling and provides opportunities for new sorts of small-group activities (e.g., Fleming, 2021). However, the initial dissatisfaction with online learning wasn't entirely misplaced. For example, if you need to discuss a hot-button issue, where nonverbal cues are particularly important, doing so in person is probably better than doing so virtually—if only because we can pick up more nonverbal cues in person.

Asking which is better in general, in-person teaching or online teaching, is a bit like asking which is better, taking a train or taking a plane. The correct answer is "It depends." No single teaching modality is always better than another; each has its virtues and drawbacks. For instance, large undergraduate courses may benefit from being taught entirely online, whereas small graduate courses may not (Shankar, Arora, & Binz-Scharf, 2021; see also Ortagus, 2022).

Although online teaching now seems unlikely to be entirely replaced by in-person teaching, if only because of economies of scale (Frank, 2020), the two teaching modalities may often come to be combined. Various forms of hybrid (sometimes called "blended") classes will be increasingly common (Harvard University, 2022; Henderson et al., 2022; Marcus, 2022; Seaman & Seaman, 2022). In fact, a survey conducted from Fall 2020 to Spring 2021 revealed that 68% of learners want to take courses that combine online and in-person teaching, and 48% of learners and 56% of instructors became more optimistic about combining online and in-person teaching as they gained more experience with remote instruction (McKenzie, 2021). Moreover, research findings indicate that when black, Hispanic and low-income learners take courses in a mix of online and in-person modalities (but no more than half of them online), they are more likely to complete an associate's or a bachelor's degree (D'Agostino, 2022).

Hybrid courses—and even entire Colleges and Universities built around them—may be the wave of the future (DeWitt, 2021; Schroeder, 2022; Young, 2022). Hence, it is worth considering in detail how such courses can be designed. In this chapter, I summarize a novel way to characterize hybrid courses and consider how to use different types of hybrid designs.

Four Teaching Modalities

For many, a "hybrid" course is simply a combination of in-person and online instruction. In this chapter, we will take a more nuanced approach by considering four teaching modalities and analyzing how best to combine them. The four modalities and their key characteristics are presented in Table 2.1. The columns are modes, Asynchronous versus Synchronous, and the rows are settings, In Person versus Online. As we use the term in this chapter, a hybrid course is created by combining two or more of the teaching modalities that are represented by the individual cells of the table.

Table 2.1 Types of Teaching Modalities

	Asynchronous	**Synchronous**
In Person	<ul><li>Individual readings and assignments</li><li>Learners do not interact</li><li>Learners do not work at any set time</li><li>Learners do not need to work at the same time that an instructor or other learners are present</li><li>Learners do not necessarily use online technology when learning</li></ul>	<ul><li>Traditional bricks-and-mortar classes</li><li>Learners and instructor meet at a specific time</li><li>Learners and instructor meet in a particular place, typically a classroom</li><li>Learners interact in real time, with each other and with the instructor</li><li>Learners do not necessarily use technology</li></ul>
Online	<ul><li>Self study that relies on a Learning Management System (LMS)</li><li>Learners rely on a LMS to access materials (e.g., recorded videos, assigned readings, and offline activities)</li><li>Learners may work at their own pace, but typically within time constraints</li><li>Learners can interact, but slowly, via a bulletin board or discussion thread</li></ul>	<ul><li>Videoconferencing classes</li><li>Learners and instructor meet at a specific time</li><li>Learners and instructor meet online, via a videoconferencing platform (either general purpose, such as Webex or Zoom, or designed just for education, such as Engageli)</li><li>Learners interact in real time, with each other and with the instructor</li></ul>

| | • Learners can interact with instructors, but slowly, via posing questions in writing or uploading a video or audio file | |

Asynchronous In-Person courses include "correspondence courses," which require learners to read textbooks or articles, complete assignments, and take tests—all on their own, at a time of their choosing. Common examples of this modality are individual project-based courses (e.g., analyzing a community on the basis of working in it) which are often given credit as "individual study" or "thesis" courses. In addition, in some cases, learners might participate in a remote lab course, such as occurs when they are shipped boxes of minerals and must analyze them in various ways.

Asynchronous Online courses are the most common version of asynchronous courses today. Good examples of such courses are the Massive Open Online Courses (MOOCs) offered by Coursera and edX. To take these courses, the learner needs a computer or smartphone and must have access to broadband internet.

Synchronous In-Person courses are the traditional courses hosted by bricks-and-mortar institutions. Such courses have live lectures and discussions and typically also include live question-and-answer sessions. A synchronous in-person classroom can range from a 2-learner seminar to a 1,000-learner lecture.

Synchronous Online courses include most of those that were put online during the pandemic. Initially, instructors may have simply tried to give their standard lectures into a camera, but many soon adapted and began to take advantage of features such as instant polling (with immediate feedback on the results) and breakout rooms.

These four modalities can be used in pairs (and there are six unique pairs), or three can be used together (and there are four unique combinations of three), or all four can be used together. Thus, the four modalities can be combined to produce 11 different types of hybrid classes. In the remainder of this chapter, we consider which combination is appropriate for a given purpose in a given context.

Selecting Modalities: Learning Objectives, Constraints, and Resources

There is no single "best" combination of modalities. The most appropriate combination depends on three types of factors.

Learning objectives are crucial because the appropriate hybrid combination depends in part on the specific types of knowledge or skills that learners need to acquire. For example, you might use one set of teaching modalities to provide a general orientation to a field and another to teach the writing skills that are used in one aspect of that field.

Constraints are factors that must be taken into account and requirements that must be met. We recognize two sorts of such constraints: On the one hand, you, as an instructor and/or course designer, have constraints. For example, such constraints can include your budget (e.g., for producing educational materials) and the number of learners you must accommodate in the course. On the other hand, the learners also have constraints, such as the times of day they can take courses and how easily they can travel to a campus.

Resources are what you and the learners have that can be drawn upon in the course. Resources are prerequisites: You must have them in order to be able to use a specific modality in a particular way. Again, there are two sorts of resources: On the one hand, some resources bear on the ease of creating and delivering the course. For example, you might have appropriate space in buildings and access to a good video conferencing platform and Learning Management System (LMS). On the other hand, the learners have specific resources that can be drawn upon in the course. For example, they may have computers, smartphones, access to broadband, and access to a digital library.

The goal is to select a combination of teaching modalities that takes into account all three types of factors. In order to choose a given modality, we need to specify when it is appropriate for specific types of learning objectives, constraints, and resources. Thus, the next step is to consider key factors that affect the modalities. (Note: In what follows, I have only included factors that distinguish the modalities; I've not included factors that all share, such as the constraint of needing a qualified course designer or the resource of having the means to recruit appropriate learners.)

In Table 2.2, a dark cell indicates that the factor is necessary or appropriate for the modality, and an empty cell indicates that the factor is either not appropriate or simply irrelevant (e.g., having access to a lecture hall and small meeting rooms is not relevant for the online modalities or the Asynchronous In-Person modality, but is clearly necessary for the Synchronous In-Person modality).

Table 2.2 Factors that Affect Which Teaching Modalities Are Appropriate

	Asynchronous In Person	Asynchronous Online	Synchronous In Person	Synchronous Online
I. Learning Objective Factors				
Learners need rapid feedback			■	■
Instructor needs rapid feedback			■	■
Need to read nonverbal cues			■	
Spontaneous Exploration			■	■
Experiential learning	■		■	
Object manipulation	■		■	
Complex, scaffolded material	■	■	■	■
II. Constraints				
Transition Time	■	■		■
Flexible scheduling	■	■		

Limited physical space				
Scaling				
Cost				
III. Resources				
Motivation and support				
Learner bonding				
Instructor relationship				
Data collection				
Breakout groups				
Tech resources				

Let's now consider these factors, one at a time.

Learning Objective Factors

The first step is to consider your learning objectives and what is required to achieve them. The following factors can help or hinder the learners from achieving these objectives in the different teaching modalities.

- *Rapid learner feedback.* Do your learning objectives involve acquiring a new skill or applying new knowledge in specific ways? If so, then rapid learner feedback is especially relevant. Do your learning objectives require learners to grasp new foundational material, which they may find difficult and hence fail to grasp initially? If so, again, rapid learner feedback is especially relevant. In general, interacting in real time in either of the synchronous modalities allows instructors to provide rapid feedback to learners and vice versa. In contrast, questions and comments that need to be submitted asynchronously typically are not addressed quickly.

- *Rapid instructor feedback.* Do your learning objectives vary in how challenging they are so that you are likely to need to adjust your pace for different material? Do your learners have a range of levels of relevant knowledge or skill? If so, you need a modality that allows you to adjust the level of a lecture or discussion based on questions or comments you receive. This ability to respond and adapt is important for keeping learners engaged (Nguyen, 2021). The synchronous modalities have a clear edge here. Instruction in the asynchronous modalities cannot be adjusted on the fly.
- *Reading nonverbal cues.* Does your learning objective involve hot-button issues? Hot-button issues can evoke strong emotions, which can disrupt the mental processes that underlie learning (McGaugh, 2003). If so, the modality should allow you to notice non-verbal cues from learners and manage the discussion so that emotions do not overwhelm the learning process. At present, being in the same physical room is by far the best way to notice "body language" and other nonverbal cues. In particular, we humans unconsciously perceive "microexpressions" (such as a twitch of an eyebrow or tightening of the jaw), which convey much emotion—and require high resolution to detect (Ekman, 2003). In general, we have only limited ability to notice such non-verbal cues online, given the resolution limits of screens (which are even more severe if learners are taking courses on their smartphones). Thus, the Synchronous In-Person modality clearly has an edge in this situation.
- *Spontaneous exploration.* Is your learning objective relatively broad and requires being fleshed out by exploring different aspects of it? Such exploration requires that learners and instructors can pose questions that lead a discussion to take a new turn. This is difficult in the asynchronous modalities, given the time delays that are built into any interaction. Because events unfold in real time in the

synchronous modalities, learners can ask questions or make comments that enrich the discussion—which can be very motivating to learners.

- *Ease of experiential learning.* Does your learning objective rely on a large experiential learning project? If so, then having unstructured time is important. This is a major strength of the Asynchronous In-Person modality: Learners can engage in activities and projects independently, drawing on many different sorts of resources (e.g., in their community) and working at their own pace. None of the other modalities are tailored for such large-scale experiential learning. However, some forms of experiential learning (particularly demonstrations that can be delivered online) can be done effectively in synchronous classes, but in general, the other three teaching modalities do not facilitate experiences outside of formal classroom settings.
- *Object manipulation.* Do learners need to actually manipulate physical objects to achieve the learning objective, such as often occurs in labs? If so, the online modalities are lacking. However, in some cases, a simulation might substitute well enough for manipulating physical objects, but in others, it may not.
- *Complex cumulative material.* Some courses (especially in Science, Technology, Engineering and Math [STEM] fields) present difficult material that builds on previous material, and thus learners can get lost if their attention lags. This is particularly a problem in synchronous classes, where there is no opportunity to go back and review what an instructor just said. However, if recorded lectures are delivered, as is common in the asynchronous modalities, learners can review the material at their own pace.

Constraint Factors

When choosing a teaching modality or modalities, the following possible constraints should be identified and respected.

- *Require minimal transition time.* Do your learners have very limited time (e.g., because they are holding down full-time jobs), and thus commuting time should be limited? If so, consider either asynchronous modality or synchronous online instruction.
- *Require flexible scheduling.* Do your learners have obligations during the day that would interfere with their taking a scheduled class? If so, consider either of the asynchronous modalities, which allow learners to take lessons at a time of their choosing (usually within boundaries, set by due dates for assignments and the like).
- *Limited physical space.* Not having access to an appropriate lecture hall limits the possibility of providing a Synchronous In-Person course; similarly, not having access to small meeting rooms limits the possibility of providing active learning in breakout groups in a Synchronous In-Person course.
- *East of scaling.* Is one of your constraints that you need to teach a large group of learners? For the Asynchronous Online modality, Massive Open Online Courses (MOOCs) have been able to grow to enormous numbers (Shah, 2020—however, note that relatively few learners actually complete these courses, Lederman, 2019). And there are no clear limits to how many learners can participate individually in the Asynchronous In-Person modality. Similarly, for the Synchronous Online modality, instructors can, in principle, deliver lectures to an open-ended number of learners, and even very large classes can then be broken down into small breakout groups. In sharp contrast, scaling is difficult in the Synchronous In-Person modality, given the limited number and sizes of classrooms.

- *Cost.* How severe a constraint is your budget? What sort of financial resources do your learners have? From the instructor or course designer's side, do new materials need to be created just for a particular course, or can existing materials (e.g., books, reprints of articles) be used? From the learner's side, are the instructional materials available through a library or online, or do they require buying an expensive textbook? The Asynchronous In-Person modality typically is the least expensive from all perspectives. In contrast, for the two online modalities, the instructor or course designer's costs can vary from minimal (if available materials are used) to very expensive (if elaborate "Interactive Learning Objects" are created). From the learner's side, costs can be high if a computer and broadband are necessary, and relatively high even if only a smartphone is required. For the Synchronous In-Person modality, physical classrooms, and the buildings they are in, must be maintained—which is not a trivial expense. In short, the asynchronous modalities tend to be less expensive (both to produce and to consume) than the synchronous ones, but a mix of modalities might be most cost-effective, for example, by using the asynchronous modalities for content delivery and the synchronous ones for most active learning (Kosslyn, 2023).

Resource Factors

Lastly, if you have the following resources, they open up specific possibilities, as noted.

- *External motivation and support.* If your learners require considerable external motivation and support, the two asynchronous modalities are lacking. In contrast, either synchronous modality allows the instructor to pick up on cues that indicate flagging motivation and to be able to intervene rapidly (especially when classes are small). This is

particularly the case when instructors or coaches conduct office hours (i.e., one-on-one or small group individual sessions outside of class). Moreover, the synchronous modalities give learners opportunities to support each other.
- *Learner bonding.* Similarly, learners are more likely to stick with their studies and master the learning objectives if they bond with other learners (Hausmann, Schofield & Woods, 2007). To promote this, your mix of teaching modalities should allow learners to interact at least some of the time, such as by including small breakout groups. Clearly, there are no such opportunities in Asynchronous In-Person teaching, and there are minimal such opportunities with Asynchronous Online teaching (although learners may interact asynchronously via bulletin boards and discussion threads, this is slow and relatively anonymous). Both of the synchronous modalities provide opportunities for learners to get to know each other, particularly if they meet often in small groups.
- *Relationship with instructor.* Another factor that promotes learner success is a relationship with the instructor. Instructors sometimes evolve into mentors, but even when they don't, they can still be a significant source of assistance and wisdom. Having a good relationship with an instructor is correlated with succeeding in school (Crisp et al., 2017; Hagenauer & Volet, 2014; Keup & Barefoot, 2014; Salinitri, 2005). Learners rarely develop a relationship with the instructor in either asynchronous modality. The two synchronous modalities do allow learners to get to know instructors, especially if office hours are part of the program (Chaves, 2021).
- *Data collection.* Can you easily collect data on learner performance? Instruction can be improved if the instructor knows how well the learners are doing. Thus, an important resource is the ability to collect data on learner performance.

This is relatively difficult to do in either of the In-Person modalities but is relatively easy to do in both of the Online modalities.
- *Breakout groups.* Do you have access to software that allows you to easily set up breakout groups? For Synchronous Online courses, most video conferencing platforms allow instructors to set up breakout groups on the spur of the moment and/or in accordance with previously specified requirements—which can include the number of learners, the amount of time allocated to the activity, specific instructions, and even the particular learners to be assigned to each group. Similarly, in Asynchronous Online settings, the instructor can set up separate groups in advance, with members interacting asynchronously (e.g., via dedicated discussion threads in the LMS); because no physical space is used, moving learners to different parts of the space is not an issue. In contrast, there are no groups in the Asynchronous In-Person modality, and the Synchronous In-Person modality requires physical logistics to arrange separate spaces and then move learners to and from the breakout rooms.
- *Tech resources.* Do your learners have access to computers and/or smart phones that are enabled with broadband internet? If so, this opens the possibility of providing an online course. Do you have access to a digital library? If not, this is a problem for the online modalities. Do you have access to a LMS, such as Canvas, Blackboard, or Moodle? If not, this is a problem for the online modalities.

After you've gone through these three sets of factors, some of the requirements may be in tension. For example, let's say that the learning objective focuses on hot-button issues, and hence a Synchronous In-Person modality would be best, but a constraint is that most learners do not live near the college and would require hours to commute to class, and hence an online or Asynchronous In-Person modality would best.

To deal with this situation, you can parse the course so that different sessions rely on different modalities—some sessions would be Synchronous In-Person, and the others in another modality, as appropriate, given the above factors. In this case, you can try to split the difference and maximize the advantages while minimizing the drawbacks of the different modalities. In fact, you can parse each individual session and use different modalities within the same session, such as by having learners acquire the content knowledge asynchronously and then participate in synchronous online breakout groups to promote active learning.

Examples of Hybrid Designs

To make this more concrete, let us consider three examples of ways to set up hybrid courses.

Example 1: Helping Impoverished People Create New Businesses

The goal is to help impoverished people who live in rural India to build new businesses that will work in their context.

Learning Objective Factors

The overarching learning objective is "Create a viable business in rural India." Let's first consider the relevance of each factor associated with the learning objective:

- *Learners need rapid feedback.* No; there's no advantage to the synchronous modalities on this score
- *The instructor needs rapid feedback.* No; again, there's no advantage to the synchronous modalities on this score.
- *Need to read nonverbal cues.* No, this does not encourage us to use the synchronous modalities.
- *Requires spontaneous exploration.* No; this subject matter is fairly cut-and-dried, and the learning objective focuses on giving the learners specific skills. Hence, spontaneous exploration is not essential.

- *Requires extensive experiential learning.* Yes; to learn these skills, the learners need to implement the ideas. This aspect of the learning objective tilts us toward the Asynchronous In-Person modality.
- *Object manipulation.* This depends on the nature of the business. If the business involves bricks-and-mortar facilities or is focused on creating or maintaining physical products, then one of the in-person modalities needs to be included.
- *Complex cumulative material.* Yes; for these learners, the material is complex and definitely is cumulative—which favors the asynchronous modalities.

Constraint Factors

The following constraints should be taken into account, and their associated requirements should be met:

- *Require minimal transition time.* Yes, these learners are working hard to survive and cannot be expected to go substantial distances to an institution to study.
- *Require flexible scheduling.* Yes, these learners need to work around their taxing daily lives.
- *Physical space.* Is a lecture hall available? No, this isn't relevant if the course won't be offered in a Synchronous In-Person modality. Are small meeting rooms available? No, but—again—this is only relevant if we want to offer the course in a Synchronous In-Person modality. Given the constraints of transition time and flexible scheduling, this modality is not optimal in any event.
- *Ease of scaling.* To have an impact, this program must scale. Scaling is easiest for the Asynchronous Online and the Synchronous Online modalities.
- *Cost.* The learners have little money, but let's assume that program production is adequately funded.

Resource Factors

Let's assume that the following resources are available; which ones are relevant?

- *External motivation and support.* Yes, these learners are going to need help. Thus, a purely Asynchronous In-Person modality is not sufficient. We need some additional synchronous contact.
- *Learner bonding.* Yes; although these learners are very motivated to finish the course, they need all the help they can get to persevere when they face the inevitable challenges their lives will present.
- *Relationship with instructor.* Yes; this is important as part of the motivation and support piece. Again, to do this well, some synchronous contact between learners and instructors is necessary.
- *Data collection.* Completion rates and test scores may be sufficient, which can be obtained in any modality.
- *Software that supports breakout groups available.* Yes, we assume that the course designer has access to appropriate video conferencing software.
- *Tech resources.* Computers/smartphones, broadband available? Yes, we assume that even very poor people have access to a smartphone that can be connected to the internet (e.g., at a public library or the like). Digital library? Let's assume that there is a digital library, so we can access the full range of modalities. Learning Management System? Let's assume that there is an LMS, so again, we have the capability of accessing the full range of modalities.

Hybrid Design

With these considerations in hand, we can review the characteristics of the different teaching modalities and select an appropriate combination of modalities.

Asynchronous In-Person: Inexpensive self-study materials already exist to help learners begin to create a new business. For example,

YouTube has many relevant videos that the learners can watch on their phones. In fact, there may be too many such videos of varying quality, and hence there is real value added by vetting and curating them. In addition, this modality leads us to mail hard copies of long readings to the learners. Moreover, this modality invites learners to work on projects on their own time, which is exactly what is needed here. However, this modality alone is probably not sufficient, if only because it does not afford easy ways to receive motivation and support.

Asynchronous Online: The instructor should set up a discussion board so that learners can ask questions and comment on other learners' ideas. This modality also can be used to allow learners to take part in asynchronous active learning exercises, which may rely on peer feedback.

Synchronous In-Person: This modality is not practical, given the constraints. Given the nature of the learning objective, which does not involve hot-button, highly emotional content, this is probably not a problem.

Synchronous Online: The bonding and motivational support that are possible in synchronous settings can largely be achieved online. The instructor can set up breakout groups at times of mutual convenience, even if only for 20 minutes at a time, to use active learning effectively in this modality. Moreover, this modality can be used for office hours, allowing learners to develop relationships with the instructors.

Example 2: Upskilling High-School Chemistry Teachers

Let's say that we want to design a course to help 10th-grade chemistry teachers learn the latest ways to use generative Artificial Intelligence (genAI) to teach basic chemistry.

Learning Objective Factors

The learning objective for the teachers is: "Use genAI to help teach chemistry." To guide the teachers to achieve this learning objective, we must teach them what the technology does and how they should use it to teach their learners. A lot of the instruction consists of teaching the teachers prompt engineering. Consider which of the following factors associated with the learning objective are particularly important:

- *Learners need rapid feedback.* Yes, the genAI systems are sufficiently complex that learners will make errors that need to be corrected quickly. Thus, there is an advantage to using the synchronous modalities.
- *The instructor needs rapid feedback.* Yes; again, there's an advantage to the synchronous modalities on this score.
- *Need to read nonverbal cues.* No; given that the material is not particularly "hot button," this factor does not encourage us to use the synchronous modalities.
- *Requires spontaneous exploration.* No; this subject matter is fairly cut-and-dried, and the learning objective focuses on giving the learners specific skills. Thus, spontaneous exploration is not essential.
- *Requires extensive experiential learning.* Yes, the instructor may want the option of using active learning that requires carrying out a project. This would be accomplished well by employing the Synchronous In-Person modality.
- *Object manipulation.* No; this learning objective can be achieved without having to manipulate any physical objects.
- *Complex cumulative material.* Yes; for these learners, the material is complex and cumulative—which favors the asynchronous modalities.

Constraint Factors

The following constraints should be taken into account, and their associated requirements should be met:

- *Require minimal transition time.* Yes, these learners are working hard and cannot be expected to go substantial distances to an institution to study. This constraint implies that either of the two asynchronous modalities or the Synchronous Online modality would be best.

- *Require flexible scheduling.* Yes, these learners need to work around their taxing daily lives, and hence either synchronous modality would be problematic if that was all that was available.
- *Physical space.* Is a lecture hall available? No, but this isn't relevant if the course won't be offered in a Synchronous In-Person modality. Are small meeting rooms available? No, but—again—this is only relevant if we want to offer the course in a Synchronous In-Person modality. Given the constraints of transition time and flexible scheduling, this modality is not optimal in any event.
- *Ease of scaling.* This program should scale so that it can be used for all high school chemistry teachers. Scaling is easiest for the two asynchronous modalities and the Synchronous Online modality.
- *Cost.* The learners do have some funding for this purpose, and let's assume that the program production is adequately funded.

Resource Factors

Let's assume that the following resources are available; which ones are relevant?

- *External motivation and support.* No, these learners are not going to need a lot of external motivation and support—they are highly motivated to master the technology. Thus, asynchronous modalities would be appropriate.
- *Learner bonding.* No; given how self-motivated these highly experienced learners will be, they don't need a lot of bonding with other learners to motivate them to finish the course. Again, this implies that asynchronous modalities would be appropriate.
- *Relationship with instructor.* No; this is not a critical factor for this learning objective with this learner population. Again, asynchronous modalities would be appropriate.

- *Data collection.* Completion rates and test scores may be sufficient, which can be obtained in any modality.
- *Software that supports breakout groups.* Yes, we assume that the instructor has access to appropriate video conferencing software.
- *Tech resources.* Computers/smartphones, broadband? Yes, we assume that these learners have access to computers and smartphones that can be connected to the internet at home. We also assume that they can be given accounts with an appropriate genAI provider. Digital library? Let's assume that there is a digital library, so we can access the full range of modalities. Learning Management System? Let's assume that there is an LMS, so again, we have the capability of accessing the full range of modalities.

Hybrid Design

Given this situation, and the characteristics outlined in Table 2.2, which modalities should we use to help the teachers learn how to use genAI to teach? Let's consider each in turn:

Asynchronous In-Person: This modality could be used for some of the learning, particularly active learning exercises that focus on carrying out a project. However, the need to have rapid feedback requires at least one of the synchronous modalities in addition to this one.

Asynchronous Online: This modality is appropriate because the teachers must work when they have time (not at any fixed time) and are highly motivated and comfortable learning this sort of material. The internet can be used in three ways to address the learning objective: First, the learners need to access a genAI to work with prompts and learn how best to construct lessons that draw on what the AI can do well. Second, the LMS can allow learners to access materials, post assignments, and interact via a discussion thread. Third, the learners can be directed toward resources that are available on particular websites so that they can become familiar with the AI and what it can do.

Synchronous In-Person: Given that the teachers are busy during the day (teaching their own learners), and the subject matter does not involve "hot button," emotional material, it doesn't make sense to try to hold live, in-person classes.

Synchronous Online: Given that the teachers have very busy schedules and have different background levels of expertise, this modality needs to be used just for aspects of instruction that are difficult to accomplish asynchronously. A main virtue of this modality is the ability to provide rapid feedback online. Thus, the instructor can set up infrequent, highly targeted groups to do active-learning exercises; these groups can be scheduled at a time of mutual convenience (e.g., as determined by using an online sign-up sheet). The learners can be grouped based on comparable levels of knowledge and skills, and the instructor can structure the groups so that learners use the genAI to teach each other. The instructor can adjust the level of the material for each group as appropriate, and the members will be comfortable with each other.

Example 3: Teaching Coding in a Small Residential College

These instructors and learners are in a traditional educational setting where all classes are taught in the Synchronous In-Person modality. However, for certain learning objectives, constraints, and resources at this particular college, it may not be possible to offer all instruction in person. In this example, cost constraints and the resulting lack of certain space resources lead us to consider hybrid courses.

Learning Objective Factors

The learning objective is "Master computer coding well enough to obtain summer employment."

- *Learners need rapid feedback.* Yes, learners often make errors when learning to code, and thus, there is an advantage to using the synchronous modalities.
- *The instructor needs rapid feedback.* Yes, the pace may need to be adjusted, depending on the precise material and

the learners' background. Again, there's an advantage to the synchronous modalities.
- *Need to read nonverbal cues.* No; given that the material is not particularly "hot button," this factor does not encourage us to use the synchronous modalities.
- *Requires spontaneous exploration.* No; this subject matter is fairly cut-and-dried, and the learning objective focuses on giving them specific skills. Hence, spontaneous exploration is not essential.
- *Requires extensive experiential learning.* No; however, although this is not required, the instructor might want the option of using active learning that requires carrying out a project. This would be accomplished well by employing the Asynchronous In-Person modality.
- *Object manipulation.* No; this learning objective can be achieved without having to manipulate any physical objects.
- *Complex cumulative material.* Yes; for these learners, the material is complex and definitely is cumulative—which favors the asynchronous modalities.

Constraint Factors

The following constraints should be taken into account, and their associated requirements should be met:
- *Require minimal transition time.* No; these learners are in a residential college and are used to moving to new classrooms.
- *Require flexible scheduling.* No; these learners expect to work around the college's schedule.
- *Physical space.* Is there a lecture hall? Yes, the course could be offered in a Synchronous In-Person modality. Are there small meeting rooms? No, this is a problem for the Synchronous In-Person modality. This is a direct consequence of the budgetary constraints, and indicates

that the Asynchronous In-Person or online modalities are appropriate.
- *Ease of scaling.* No; this program need not scale.
- *Cost.* The college is strapped for funds, and thus there isn't enough money to fully fund labs. This constraint implies that some Asynchronous In-Person activities are appropriate.

Resource Factors

Let's assume that the following resources are available; which ones are relevant?
- *External motivation and support.* No; these learners know that learning to code can lead to a good job and hence are highly motivated. Thus, asynchronous modalities would be appropriate.
- *Learner bonding.* No; given how self-motivated these learners are, they don't need a lot of bonding with other learners to motivate them to finish the course. Again, this implies that asynchronous modalities would be appropriate.
- *Relationship with instructor.* No; this is not a critical factor for this learning objective with this learner population. Again, asynchronous modalities would be appropriate.
- *Data collection.* If learners will be doing a lot of their work online, they (and/or their parents) will want to know that they are getting their money's worth. Thus, instructors want to collect data on learner performance to ensure that they are doing the work—and to help them (and retain them as learners) if they falter.
- *Software that supports breakout groups.* Yes, we assume that the instructor has access to appropriate video conferencing software.
- *Tech resources.* Computers/smartphones, broadband? Yes, we assume that these learners have access to computers and smartphones that can be connected to the internet at home. Digital library? Let's assume that there is a digital

library, so we can access the full range of modalities. Learning Management System? Let's assume that there is an LMS, so again, we have the capability of accessing the full range of modalities.

Hybrid Design

Given this situation and the characteristics outlined in Table 2.2, which modalities should we use to help the learners master coding? Let's consider each in turn:

Asynchronous In-Person: The course would include assignments that require learners to write code on their own time; such assignments are best done in this modality.

Asynchronous Online: Assignments, PowerPoint decks of lectures, readings, sample computer code, and videos are posted on the LMS. This is an inexpensive way to distribute materials. In addition, learners may post questions on a bulletin board, which other learners or the instructor can answer. Both the questions and answers are visible to all, thereby reducing the workload for the instructor (who doesn't have to answer the same question twice).

Synchronous In Person: Given the learning objective, constraints, and resources, Synchronous In-Person lectures, with adequate time for question-and-answer sessions, are feasible.

Synchronous Online: Given the opportunity to teach in person, there is no need to deliver lectures online—the lower resolution on the screen can obscure some nonverbal signals, which reduces the quality of some feedback. However, the lack of space for small discussion groups implies that such groups should be offered via video conferencing. Such groups can help learners with aspects of the skill they find most difficult; such feedback is especially useful if it is provided in real time. Thus, having learners meet in small groups to work on coding can be helpful, especially if the groups are composed of learners at comparable levels. Moreover, various data—such as the relative amount of time that different learners talk or contribute to shared documents and projects—

can be collected automatically in such sessions, which can help the instructor to identify and then address academic problems.

Conclusions

Hybrid courses can come in many different forms, depending on how the four basic teaching modalities are combined. Different combinations of modalities—and hence different forms of hybrid courses—are more or less appropriate in different circumstances. In particular, the nature of the learning objectives, constraints, and resources can guide an instructor to select the appropriate combination of teaching modalities.

As noted earlier, in some cases, there may be tension between different factors. One way to deal with this tension is to parse the course so that different modalities are used for different aspects. For example, you may decide to use different modalities for lecturing versus problem-based-learning exercises. But this may not always be possible. In situations where you have to choose, it may be necessary to emphasize some of the factors over others. For example, cost may simply be more important than some aspects of good pedagogy—if the funds are not available, they are not available.

In short, although in this chapter I have offered a set of heuristics that can guide you, human judgment is still necessary. It is up to the instructor, who knows the institution and learners, to consider the likely tradeoffs among some of the factors. Nevertheless, the present approach structures the decisions and makes the tradeoffs more transparent than simply acting on intuition alone. This transparency can facilitate not only making informed decisions but also communicating them to all stakeholders.

References

Chaves, S. (2021, March 11). I hid my personal life from my learners. Now they see it all — and I love it. *Washington Post*: https://www.washingtonpost.com/outlook/2021/03/11/zoom-teaching-school-personal-connection/

Crisp, G., Baker, V. L., Griffin, K. A., Lunsford, L. G., & Pifer, M.J. (2017). Mentoring undergraduate learners. *ASHE Higher Education Report, 43*, 105-117.

D'Agostino, S. (2022, 1 Sept). Completion boost for 2-year students who take (some) online courses. Inside Higher Ed, https://www.insidehighered.com/news/2022/09/01/study-links-completion-gains-taking-some-online-courses?utm_source=Inside+Higher+Ed&utm_campaign=463692c41c-SL_SS_Civitas_20220914&utm_medium=email&utm_term=0_1fcbc04421-463692c41c-236913270

DeWitt, P. (2021, March 3). Will the hybrid school concept continue after Covid-19? *EdWeek*: https://www.edweek.org/leadership/opinion-will-the-hybrid-school-concept-continue-after-covid/2021/03?utm_source=newsletter&utm_medium=email&utm_campaign=newsletter_axiosfutureofwork&stream=future

DeWitt, P. (2021, March 3). Will the hybrid school concept continue after COVID-19? *Education Week*, *h*ttps://www.edweek.org/leadership/opinion-will-the-hybrid-school-concept-continue-after-covid/2021/03

Ekman, P. (2003). *Emotions revealed: Recognizing faces and feelings to improve communication and emotional life.* New York: Henry Holt and Co.

Fleming, N. (2020, April 24). Why are some kids thriving during remote learning? *Edutopia*: https://www.edutopia.org/article/why-are-some-kids-thriving-during-remote-learning

Frank, R. H. (2020, June 5). Don't kid yourself: Online lectures are here to stay. *New York Times*: https://www.nytimes.com/2020/06/05/business/online-learning-winner-coronavirus.html

Hagenauer, G., & Volet, S. E. (2014). Teacher–learner relationship at university: an important yet under-researched field, *Oxford Review of Education, 40*, 370-388, DOI: 10.1080/03054985.2014.921613

Harvard University (2022). *Report of the Harvard Future of Teaching and Learning Task Force.* https://ftltaskforce.harvard.edu/files/future-teaching-learning/files/harvard_ftl_final_3.8.22_2.pdf;

Hausmann, L.R.M., Schofield, J.W., & Woods, R.L. (2007). Sense of belonging as a predictor of intentions to persist among African American and White first-year college learners. *Research in Higher Education, 48*, 803-839.

Henderson, D., Jackson, D., Kaiser, D., Kothari, S.P., & Sarma, S. (2022). *Ideas for designing an affordable new educational institution.* Cambridge, MA: The Abdul Latif Jameel World Education Lab, MIT;

Hobbs, T. D., & Hawkins, L. (2020, June 5). The results are in for remote learning: It didn't work. *Wall Street Journal*: https://www.wsj.com/articles/schools-coronavirus-remote-learning-lockdown-tech-11591375078

Keup, J. R., & Barefoot, B. O. (2005). Learning how to be a successful learner: exploring the impact of first-year seminars on learner outcomes. *Journal of the First-Year Experience & Learners in Transition, 17*, 11–47.

Kosslyn, S. M. (2023). *Active learning with AI: A practical guide.* Boston, MA: Alinea Learning.

Lederman, D. (2019, Jan 16). Why MOOCs didn't work in 3 data points. *Inside Higher Ed*: https://www.insidehighered.com/digital-learning/article/2019/01/16/study-offers-data-show-moocs-didnt-achieve-their-goals

Marcus, J. (2022). What researchers learned about online education during the pandemic. *The Hechinger Report*, https://hechingerreport.org/what-researchers-learned-about-online-higher-education-during-the-pandemic/

McGaugh, J.L. (2003). *Memory and emotion: The making of lasting memories*. New York: Columbia University Press.

McKenzie, L. (2021, April 27). Students want online learning options post-pandemic. *Inside Higher Ed*, https://www.insidehighered.com/news/2021/04/27/survey-reveals-positive-outlook-online-instruction-post-pandemic

Nguyễn, C. T. (2021, March 11). Zoom classes felt like teaching into a void—until I told my learners why. *Washington Post*: https://www.washingtonpost.com/outlook/zoom-classes-felt-like-teaching-into-a-void--until-i-told-my-learners-why/2021/03/11/024afb2c-81e5-11eb-81db-b02f0398f49a_story.html

Ortagus, J.C. (2022). *Digitally divided: The varying impacts of online enrollment on degree completion*. Institute of Higher Education, University of Florida: Working Paper 2201.

Salinitri, G. (2005). The effects of formal mentoring on the retention rates for first-year, low achieving learners. *Canadian Journal of Education, 24*, 853-873.

Schroeder, R. (2022, Sept 21). Imagine we are starting a university now. *Inside Higher Ed*, https://www.insidehighered.com/digital-learning/blogs/online-trending-now/imagine-we-are-starting-university-now

Seaman, J.E., & Seaman, J. (2022). *Turning point for digital curricula: Educational resources in US higher education, 2022.* Bay Area Analytics, https://www.bayviewanalytics.com/reports/turningpointdigitalcurricula.pdf

Shah, D. (2020, Nov 30). By the numbers: MOOCs in 2020. *The Report by Class Central.* https://www.classcentral.com/report/mooc-stats-2020/

Shankar, K., Arora, P., & and Binz-Scharf, M. C.. (2021). Evidence on online higher education: The promise of COVID-19 pandemic data. *Management and Labour Studies,* 1–8. DOI: 10.1177/0258042X211064783

Singer, N. (2021, April 11). Online schools are here to stay, even after the pandemic. *New York Times:* https://www.nytimes.com/2021/04/11/technology/remote-learning-online-school.html?campaign_id=9&emc=edit_nn_20210412&instance_id=29131&nl=the-morning&regi_id=89956178&segment_id=55394&te=1&user_id=689fde9a0c6c905c68e8a4896013cee2

Young, J. R. (2022, Sept 28). MIT Professors propose a new kind of university for post-COVID era. *EdSurge.* https://www.edsurge.com/news/2022-09-28-mit-professors-propose-a-new-kind-of-university-for-post-covid-era#:~:text=In%202016%2C%20then%2DMIT%20dean,and%20partnered%20with%2090%20organizations.

Chapter 3

Maria Anguiano

The Equity Imperative: Putting Learners' Needs at the Heart of Higher Education Design

Abstract
Every day, learners have to navigate a college system that was not designed for them. We ask them to follow our rules and play our game, yet this design has disproportionately affected students of color and students experiencing poverty. It is time to change how we structure higher education opportunities to ensure that learners their lives, needs, and dreams are at the heart of every design decision.

"Talent is equally distributed; opportunity is not."

Over the last few decades, we have seen a growth in the number of students who are college ready and want to pursue a college degree. However, although thousands more students enter college, only about half are completing. One of the reasons for this poor completion rate has to do with the rigid and linear design of the US higher education system. Many students are navigating a college system that was not designed with their circumstances in mind. There are a series of implicit rules built into the college navigation system, and students are asked to navigate it and play "the game," but without being told what the rules are or what the game is. This system especially harms first-generation students, students of color, and those experiencing poverty because they don't typically have the support system to help them navigate these implicit rules or "hidden curriculum" (as we shall discuss shortly).

In this chapter, we lay the groundwork for why a hybrid college program effectively solves some of the inequities endemic within the current higher education design. We start by exploring the new demographics of higher education as well as the existing higher education operating framework and its negative impact on college completion rates. We also examine the student experience from an equity lens, considering how some elements of the current design impede student success. Additive structures, while well-intentioned, will not adequately correct design barriers. Thus, we also explore how to deconstruct the current design and rebuild with an equity mindset, demonstrating why and how a hybrid college program puts learners' needs at the heart of an equity-centered design.

Who Are We Serving?

The demographics of college campuses have changed dramatically in the last 30 years. They are more diverse than ever, and it is common for an institution to track demographic data as a key indicator of DEI (Diversity, Equity and Inclusion) efforts. California's higher education institutions illustrate the expanding diversity of college campuses:

Table 3.1 California University Demographics

University of California (UC) Demographics	California State University (CSU)* Demographics
<ul><li>41% of UC undergrads are first-generation students</li><li>49% of UC first-generation students are African American, Latino/Chicano, or American Indian</li><li>60% of UC first-generation students are from lower-income households</li></ul>	<ul><li>CSU is the nation's largest public university</li><li>Nearly half of CSU students are from under-represented groups (URG)</li><li>Half of CSU undergraduates receive Pell grants</li><li>Nearly 33% of CSU undergraduates are first-generation students</li></ul>

Though many campuses are doing a great job at diversifying their student population, they are not necessarily doing a great job at getting their students to the finish line. One of the reasons for this is that most college structures continue to revolve around serving what used to be described as the traditional student. A "traditional" student could be defined as an 18–24-year-old who is a dependent, full-time student working fewer than 16 paid hours a week. This demographic is what most people think of when they hear the words "college student." It turns out, however, that only 1 in 4 current college-goers actually fit that description.

When a new cohort of students get to their first day of college, they are immediately bombarded with new information and rapid changes. They are adapting not only to college-level academics, expectations, and course pedagogy but also to the broader context of the college experience. For some, it is immersive. They live on or near campus. They can afford to live away from home for the first time, and their commute consists of walking from the dorm to the classroom to the dining hall. They are free to focus their time on academics, building friendships, and their extracurricular activities. These students may work limited hours for extra spending money, but the work is often an enhancement to the experience rather than a critical need. As noted previously, this profile represents only 25% of current college-goers, those that are dependents, full-time students, and working fewer than 16 paid hours a week.

The majority of students (75%) have a multitude of responsibilities, age ranges, and socioeconomic circumstances. For these students attending college is only possible through outside employment. They may live at home with their parents, or they may have their own home with their own children. They may live over an hour away from campus, causing a long commute. That means they have to schedule classes, work groups, and study time around work and home responsibilities. These learners may be more likely to be first-generation students of color, students experiencing poverty, working students, student parents, and students older than 24. The college experience of these modern students looks wildly different than that of their traditional counterparts.

Given the increased diversity in the types of students enrolled in colleges and universities, we have made great strides on the access front. Yet access is not enough. Consider the following sobering statistics:

- Less than half of college students graduate on time, and only 62% of those attempting this path graduate within six years.
- Three-quarters of college dropouts are first-generation college students, and more than two-thirds of college dropouts are low-income students with family-adjusted gross income (AGI) under $50,000.
- High-income students with a family AGI of $100,000 or higher are 50% more likely to graduate than low-income students.

Something is clearly amiss, especially given that our society has made postsecondary education a key to social mobility. In order for us to make that a reality for all, we have to ensure that colleges and universities are structured in a way that all students can thrive. It's time to take a deep look at how universities and colleges are operating and how they are serving their students. It is time to change how we structure higher education opportunities to ensure that learners, their lives, needs, and dreams are at the heart of every design decision; that we do not just provide "access" but rather an environment and the types of programs where modern students can thrive.

The Artificial Barriers our Students Must Face

Access to higher education has to mean more than merely a ticket in the door. We must proactively seek to support these learners more, addressing the whole of their existence rather than assuming or expecting that they will function like the students of generations past. If the system was designed for a particular student profile, and the majority of students no longer fit that profile, we must also ask if that design is even relevant now. We must actively evolve the design to better fit our modern students and enable their success.

How do we design college for this new majority? This is where equity-centered design comes into play. As we examine the holistic college experience and the levers that we have to pull to enable student success, we have to move beyond focusing on the in-person course schedule and on-campus student life. While those are certainly important, we must take into consideration the broader context of challenges and responsibilities many learners face. For these learners, student success depends on balancing all of the various, and often competing and disjointed, aspects of life. They do not have the option of wearing a single hat at a given time in their experience. These individuals are not just "students" but also simultaneously "children," "siblings," "grandchildren," "parents," and "employees," among others. It is our responsibility to recognize the context in which our learners join class, study, take exams, and engage in campus life. Equity-centered design requires exploring these contextual differences and designing an experience that provides a supportive environment for all. Doing so means that we need to get more personalized and granular at providing support for the diversity of our students' needs. It also means, however, fundamentally changing the "sacred cow" operating structures of colleges and universities.

There are many examples of our higher education systems not working for modern learners. The rigidity of a class schedule with fully in-person courses is only one such example. Let's take, for example, a working student that has a mandatory Tuesday/Thursday at 10 am one semester and then a Monday/Wednesday class at 2 pm the next semester. How can they keep the consistent work schedule their employer requires? What if they could create their schedule to ensure their required courses all fit within their work schedule? What if they could take these courses asynchronously online? We recognize that there are sound pedagogical reasons for much of the current design, yet as our student population's needs change, we must also consider if the design serves our modern learners who need more flexibility from our institutions to successfully navigate through their post-secondary education.

The example above is an ***explicit curriculum*** issue that can be redesigned. We also need to consider the "***hidden curriculum.***"

The term "hidden curriculum" refers to the "shadowy, ill-defined" rules implicitly embedded in higher education. Learners receive a formal or stated curriculum, including the courses they take, the syllabi provided by faculty, etc. The hidden curriculum refers to the unwritten, informal rules that govern the broader context or college atmosphere surrounding these courses. These "rules of the game," simultaneously vague and murky, often come as a complete surprise to first-generation students.

In other words, the hidden curriculum is a set of expectations that students are supposed to follow, yet these rules are not expressly communicated or taught. The hidden curriculum is "hidden" because it is usually unacknowledged or unexamined and is accepted as the status quo. Those with prior knowledge of the rules consider them to be natural and universal, and following them is simply "how it's done."

The students who know and understand these unspoken rules and tacit norms are prepared to succeed in college because they already know the rules, and the students with no or little prior knowledge are not even aware of when they are breaking the rules or how to use the rules to their advantage.

Consider a range of "normal" college activities:
- Navigating a university library
- Discussing financial aid matters
- Conversing with faculty
- Attending office hours
- Networking with peers
- Finding an internship
- Interacting with individuals of different cultural and socioeconomic backgrounds

Participating in Extracurricular Activities

To the "traditional" college students, these activities may seem routine, even mundane, natural and unquestioned elements of the college experience. But for a first-generation student, many of these activities are more akin to learning a foreign language.

The initial year of college is, of course, an adjustment for all students. Part of the overall experience is learning to navigate education at the college level. However, not all transitions into college learning are created equal. Learners whose parents attended college have a distinct advantage as their parents would have already navigated this hidden curriculum and can readily share insights and strategies of how to negotiate the new environment successfully. Simply having a parent acknowledge that these shadowy structures exist or share their own stories will validate the student's experience. Knowing that their parents successfully encountered these same structures undoubtedly strengthens confidence in their own ability to succeed. In fact, learners with parents who attended college "routinely took for granted the procedural and content-specific guidance their parents continued to provide." Research also demonstrates that feeling ill-prepared for college can cause "considerable psychological strain in the first weeks and months of college," a feature particularly common for first-generation students unfamiliar with the rules of this particular game and without parents to understand, and then assuage, the initial discomfort.

Many aspects of the hidden curriculum require more than mere knowledge of the system but the confidence to navigate it. A student may be told that office hours are available but lack the confidence to approach a faculty member or struggle with how to articulate a question or need. Similarly, a student may be aware that a particular service is available, such as career counseling, but not necessarily understand the value of the service or how to leverage the opportunity best. These skills will, of course, develop over time, but for learners also balancing work commitments and home responsibilities while still adapting to the formal curriculum and college-level academics, not understanding these elements of the hidden curriculum may have an even greater impact. Without the guidance of parents or outside support system, first-generation students will most often navigate the hidden curriculum through trial and error, causing additional strain and compromising their ability to succeed.

If this initial transition period goes poorly, first-generation students typically blame themselves, questioning whether they belong at the institutions, whereas learners whose parents attended college are "more apt to scrutinize the institution and ask whether it could do more to serve them." Universities must understand these attribution gaps and how first-generation learners are more likely internalize the struggles they face. These issues lie at the core of the equity imperative.

Well-Intentioned but Inadequate Responses

Institutions have been aware of this hidden curriculum for some time, and research has demonstrated the need for additional support for first-generation students. As with DEI, higher education institutions across the country are rightly making investments in these areas. Traditional responses generally include additive programs or support measures tacked on to existing structures. Such programs and support might include:

- Websites dedicated to first-generation students
- College introductory courses to first-generation students
- Summer programs
- Social events
- First-generation centers
- First-generation communities
- Glossaries of college terms

These programs uncover aspects of the hidden curriculum and do, in fact, offer needed support. However, each of the programs noted above is an additive solution that adds to the institution's cost structure; a new program tacked on to the existing design, which remains unchanged. These additive solutions are often not scalable and do not get to the core fundamentals of the actual challenges facing an ever-greater number of our students.

The reality is that these programs will do little for learners who must still work 20-30 hours each week or have a long commute from home to work to school. An introductory course or website may explain the benefits of office hours, but the service provides little value if a student cannot attend because of work. Exposing the hidden curriculum alone does not actually support the learner having trouble scheduling classes because of work and home demands. Similarly, while building a network and community around our modern students is important, if their schedules impede active involvement, we must question the efficacy of the program. Additive supports and structures, while helpful, do NOT correct for the structural design issues facing higher education.

In the following section, we will deconstruct the current higher education design and discuss how a hybrid approach to learning can be a tool to support students with navigating hidden curriculums and equitable outcomes at scale.

Deconstructing Current Design

Research is clear on the existence of this hidden curriculum and the unique needs of first-generation students, working students, students of color, and students experiencing poverty, yet higher education has struggled with how to operationalize the necessary changes and mobilize to meet these needs successfully. Instead of trying to fit first-generation students or students of color into these existing structures that are clearly not designed for them, we suggest that there is an equity imperative and even moral mandate to deconstruct the current design.

It is not sufficient to merely illuminate the hidden curriculum. We must deconstruct the higher education experience from the core and design with an equity mindset so that the equity lens infuses every design decision. In this way, the hidden curriculum barrier is neutralized by explicitly embedding it into the program. We need to create an experience that addresses the whole person, not merely design a plug-in program that does little to address the underlying structures of inequity. Only in this way will we be able to solve inequality systematically.

While institutions continue to champion the importance of equity, actually achieving this equity will require deconstructing and then rebuilding from the ground up with an equity lens. This process will require both trust and humility. It will require difficult, nuanced conversations, an analysis of accepted pedagogy, and a willingness actually to reexamine current practices. It will require a true collaboration among academic, administrative, and student-facing departments. The Academic Senate must be invested and open to this process. University leaders must create safe spaces for their teams to reflect on these areas, examining whether our current structures serve *all* students well.

Elements of Equity-Centered Design

An equity-centered approach requires both a macro and micro assessment of student needs. It requires examining the actual academic coursework and broader support environment with an equity lens. The following examples illustrate the type of questioning and analysis the equity lens requires.

Course Design

Particular focus must be given to gateway courses. Research demonstrates that these courses may serve as gatekeepers for URM and low-income students. These courses are required to attain a degree and yet have been found to contribute to equity gaps in retention and completion rates. If we are invested in the equity imperative and are seeing disparities in how different types of students excel or fall behind in these foundational courses, we must ask why and how we can improve. Is it an issue of preparation and readiness for college-level academics? Is it the difficulty of the content or the delivery method? How can we best address the gaps?

Flexibility of the Overall Experience

Our increasing number of modern students require a higher level of flexibility and support in the broader environment. If 3 in 4 students are working 16 hours per week, living at home and commuting to school, or juggling outside home responsibilities, we must consider how we can build the flexibility to support success. Flexible structures supporting equity might include:

Academics
- *Flexibility of modality and course load.* Hybrid courses could allow students to choose where and when to take their courses in a way that fits their schedule, ramping up to part-time and full-time seamlessly based on their particular needs at any given time.
- *Online access.* Course availability 24/7, anytime, anywhere within a digital platform is important for working students with family responsibilities.
- *Start-anytime.* Could colleges provide more opportunities for students to start whenever they were ready? Remove the timing barriers to starting courses, and create the ability for students to start their path.

To illustrate the impact of changing the modality and constraints within which a course is offered, consider Arizona State University's Earned Admissions Program powered by its Universal Learning Courses. These courses are first-year ASU college courses offered online and open to everyone. ULCs enable learners to test the college waters by earning college credit for a fraction of the cost: $25 to register and $400 only if they are satisfied with their grade. Once learners complete their required ULC courses with a 2.75 GPA or higher, Earned Admission allows them to gain admission into ASU or transfer their credits to any institution that accepts ASU credits. The Earned Admissions college pathway has provided more than 4,000 students access to the nation's most innovative degree programs. This number is rapidly growing and affirms that earned admission students belong at ASU. The early data demonstrate that they are thriving at ASU.

Figure 3.2 ASU's Earned Admissions Program

ASU's Universal Learning Courses		
ASU's Universal Learner Courses (ULCs) provide an innovative example of an equity-centered design. ULCs are a selection of first-year college courses offered online at ASU that are open to everyone. Through ULCs, individuals can test the college waters, earn college credit for a fraction of the cost and pay only if they pass the course. Learners receive a transcript showing their completed courses. ULCs open new opportunities for high school learners, transfer students, and gap year learners.		
Defining Characteristics	**Description**	**Equity-Centered Design**
Start Anytime	Learners choose from 50+ for-credit courses, all available online, with many offered as self-paced. Individuals pay only $25 to start.	Offers flexibility of when learner can take it
Universal Eligibility	No Transcripts are needed. No application is required. No GPA thresholds.	No barrier to entry
No penalty for failure	Learners pay $400 for the course only if they successfully pass with a "C" or higher. The total course cost is $425.	Low risk (learners can try again and again)
ASU Admission	If a learner completes courses with a 2.75 GPA or higher.	Creates multiple pathways into university

Student Support Systems

- *Career focus.* While this is part of many college experiences, it is usually only for those who know to pursue this path and is part of the "hidden curriculum." Colleges can make this curriculum explicit by creating a mechanism for students to engage in these opportunities. It's important these be embedded as part of the curriculum for ALL students, not just some or as part of an optional program. The key to success in this area is the systemic embeddedness of career success curriculum and work opportunities with every student provided opportunities as part of their official college experience. Leaving it to chance disadvantages modern students who already have a significant workload outside of their curricular responsibilities. These programs also allow students who already have to work to leverage this time into a career-enhancing experience. It also ensures that career preparedness is a key part of the college experience for all students.

If career experiences are to be designed to be a core part of every student's experience, they must be scalable, and this is where the hybrid design should be leveraged. Recognizing the limited time available for many modern students and the working professionals participating, these experiences must be highly curated with partner organizations and professionals that share a common vision for active mentorship and understand the constraints for all. These experiences can be tailored to leverage online components for more general training and hands-on training that is tailored to a learner's specific talents, skills, and interests.

- *Cohorts.* Creation of learner cohorts for both academic and emotional support. Most colleges assume that these communities form through the dorm experience for students. Many commuters are left to fend for themselves in creating supportive communities. Not living on campus does not mean that it is not possible to build a tight-knit community. However, they must be developed intentionally, and institutions can build them explicitly by assigning students to a cohort when they start and developing programming for these cohorts. Again, the key here is to embed the cohorts as an explicit part of the curriculum for all students. This ensures that this is an inclusive program that does not exclude any segments of the student body and is not just an additive structure that creates additional costs for a college and is subject to elimination.

- *Coaches.* Eliminate the need to navigate a labyrinth of services by assigning coaches to students who serve as navigators and advocates, personally connecting with and understanding the environment of a student's education, removing roadblocks, and providing support at all levels to enable the student's success. This does not have to be a large expense for a college to implement this coaching type. An example of a lean way to embed this type of equity-centered support is ASU's award-winning Student Success Center (SSC). SSC provides ASU students access and opportunities to succeed through peer coaching in cohort and non-cohort-based models. Success coaching empowers students to thrive both inside and outside the classroom, and it's customized to individual interests, strengths, and needs. Demonstrating how the right person at the right time can change a life, Success coaches work with students on everything from transition (adjusting to college life) to transformation (realizing potential and dreams). Success coaches answer questions about college life and provide insider tips and advice on academics, getting involved, finding scholarships, and more. This empowers the student employees and professional staff to gain cultural competence through continued training and personal reflection so that continuous improvement is integral to the way students are served and supported.

Creating a Hybrid College Model

The previous section describes the ingredients of an equity-centered design. However, like any good recipe, it's how you combine the ingredients that make or breaks the resulting meal.

A hybrid college structure can mix these ingredients in a way that leverages the best of flexible remote learning with the critical support structures that are best delivered in person, thereby offering an effective solution to many of the challenges discussed earlier in this chapter. How an institution chooses to combine the ingredients will, of course, depend on the local community, demographics of the student body, and available online infrastructure.

On the academic side, online course modalities offer much-needed flexibility for learners who are no longer tied to rigid course schedules that often conflict with work schedules and home responsibilities. Creating high-quality courses that are available for 24/7 access and can be started at any time with low risk allows learners the freedom and ability to design their schedules to best fit their life circumstances.

On the student support side, community building and coaching can be designed to be experienced in person. While modern learners will still require flexibility in these areas, they can be carefully designed in such a way that the limited in-person hours bring maximum results.

A college experience is so much more than attending classes and progressing toward a degree. Community and relationships add a layer of richness to the overall experience. As noted above, living off campus should not mean that a modern learner is unable to build and actively participate in a robust community. How that community is developed may look different and will require intentionality by the program architects. A cohort model actively connects students by providing intentional, in-person opportunities to ensure that the students are not navigating the online curriculum in isolation. Coaches facilitate these connections and provide a reliable touch point for students as they progress through the program and, more importantly, when they stumble or struggle.

Hybrid formats allow traditional universities to scale by creating more flexibility regarding where "college happens." Once an institution is open to a digital delivery of curriculum, it creates massive flexibility in where students learn. Hub-and-spoke campus models could be leveraged that make getting to "campus" more accessible for modern learners. Having several locations in major metro areas allow students to access campuses with a quick commute and continue to live in their local communities. As described above, these types of hybrid learning locations are effective when combined with online learning options, in-person learning communities, and success coaches to complement the experience at the satellite location.

Another chapter in this volume shares a deep dive into an equity-centered hybrid college case study, ASU Local. This program was created with a deep understanding of modern students and incorporated many of the equity-centered design elements shared in this chapter.

Conclusion

Both faculty and administrators within higher education are involved in the noble pursuit of advancing learning. A college degree can change the trajectory of a family and open opportunities for generational wealth, security, and stability. Yet in this noble mission, we must be honest with ourselves. We must be willing to confront the structures of old, the "sacred cows" of our institutions and the broader field and to replace our current lens with an equity lens. Doing so will free us to create and design new, more effective models to serve and support ALL of our students.

References

California State University. (2021). Facts about the CSU. Retrieved May 26, 2023, from https://www.calstate.edu/csu-system/about-the-csu/facts-about-the-csu/Documents/facts2021.pdf

Gable, R. (2021). The Hidden Curriculum: First Generation Students at Legacy Universities. Princeton University Press.

Kantrowitz, M. (2021, November 18). Shocking Statistics About College Graduation Rates. Forbes. Retrieved May 26, 2023, from https://www.forbes.com/sites/markkantrowitz/2021/11/18/shocking-statistics-about-college-graduation-rates/?sh=6fb80deb2b69

Koch, A., & Drake, B. (2018, November). Digging into the Disciplines I: Accounting for Failure- The Impact of Principles of Accounting Courses on Student Success and Equitable Outcomes. John N. Gardner Institute for Excellence in Undergraduate Education.

National Student Clearinghouse Research Center. (n.d.). Completing College. Retrieved May 26, 2023, from https://nscresearchcenter.org/completing-college/

Sasse, Ben. How to Really Fix American Higher Ed. The Atlantic. Retrieved May 26, 2023, from https://www.theatlantic.com/ideas/archive/2022/05/student-loans-forgiveness-higher-ed/639438/

Sambell, K., & McDowell, L. (1998). The Construction of the Hidden Curriculum: messages and meanings in the assessment of student learning. Assessment & Evaluation in Higher Education, 23(4), 391-402. DOI: 10.1080/0260293980230406

University of California. (n.d.). First-generation students. Retrieved May 26, 2023, from https://www.universityofcalifornia.edu/student-success/firstgen#:~:text=41%25%20of%20UC%20undergraduates%20are,UC%20undergraduates%20are%20first%2Dgeneration

PART 2

How to Hybrid

Kimberly Merritt, Elizabeth P. Callaghan, Stephen M. Kosslyn

Introduction: Making Hybrid Work

This second section covers the practicalities of making hybrid education work. In the first section, we explored the benefits of hybrid approaches to teaching and learning, exploring compelling reasons to embrace hybrid education and its benefits to students, educators, and society. Now, we'll examine how to put theory into practice.

Here, we provide a toolkit of strategies, techniques, and best practices for implementing hybrid education to the best effect. Our goal is to help you design, develop, and deliver effective and engaging hybrid courses and programs. We want to empower educators, administrators, and institutions to create meaningful learning experiences that meet the needs of today's diverse student populations and prepare them for the challenges of the 21st century.

The chapters in this section cover a wide range of practical topics. Here, we outline best practices for designing and delivering hybrid courses that seamlessly integrate in-person and online learning. From an administrative perspective, we summarize strategies for creating institutional support and organizational change and offer ways to assist faculty in the transition to hybrid teaching. From the classroom perspective, we describe ways to create strong connections among hybrid modalities, build strong learning communities, and use hybrid models to maximize one of education's most precious resources: direct interaction between teacher and student.

As you read the chapters in this section, we encourage you to reflect on your experiences, consider your unique teaching and learning context, and think critically about how to apply these insights to your hybrid classroom. The power of hybrid education lies in its flexibility, adaptability, and capacity for innovation. By embracing this approach, you can create transformative learning experiences that meet the needs of all learners and prepare them our rapidly changing world.

We hope these chapters will inspire you to experiment with new approaches, challenge your assumptions, and ultimately create a dynamic and engaging hybrid learning environment for students.

Chapter 4

John Katzman and Melora Sundt

An Agile University Structure for Hybrid Course Design

Abstract

Hybrid and online programs and courses require more than thoughtful learning design. They require an agile university infrastructure that seamlessly, efficiently, and effectively markets, recruits, supports, and places students and professors regardless of the modality they choose.

Introduction

Hybrid courses create optimal learning experiences. By "hybrid," we refer to teaching that includes online and on-ground (i.e., face-to-face in-person) experiences and asynchronous and synchronous experiences. When these modalities are used effectively in combination, benefits accrue, such as: (a) maximizing the use of time in- and out-of-class; (b) maximizing resources such as physical space and calendar/term time; (c) maximizing the creation of community by allowing students, faculty, and staff to connect, regardless of their location; and (d) increasing institutional resilience by reducing (where possible) the disruption of educational access by natural disasters and, yes, pandemics.

In addition to a better learning experience, online, hybrid learning offers students flexibility and convenience, but they demand changes to a university's structure and services. Based on our work implementing online and hybrid programs at top institutions across the US, we share here what it means for universities to be "agile" in the context of hybrid learning, the key principles driving that transformation, and specific changes to common administrative processes that can significantly increase agility in the long and short term.

The traditional pathway to creating hybrid programs involves encouraging individual faculty and single programs to take their programs online versus moving an entire system online. The challenges created by this path are numerous. Success relies on faculty to transform their courses–perhaps not the best use of faculty time, nor do all faculty have the knowledge and resources to make effective course transformations. When individual courses get put online one by one, we often see a lack of consistency, leading to a less coherent student experience. Faculty or even learning designer inexperience may result in design choices that do not make the best use of asynchronous and synchronous time or on-campus versus online resources. Finally, a focus on moving individual courses online often overlooks the importance of integrating student and academic support services into the online environment – services that in the on-ground environment have tripled in cost over the past twenty years (Katzman, 2017) and now cost more than instructional costs–while administrators work ever-harder to address these fast-growing student needs.

Building great online course materials is expensive and will get more so. This is not unlike the rise in cost for video games; consumer standards rise, and those standards remain in lockstep with what the most innovative companies produce -- not the majority, middle-of-the-pack creators. The push to expand hybrid offerings has set off an arms race to produce the best possible learning content as technology improves, student expectations rise, and more creative minds flock to the field of learning design (Newton, 2016). Without additional students, how do institutions pay for learning design?

Higher education is already perceived as too expensive (Walton Family Foundation, 2020), and the typical strategy for mitigating costs, described next, is untenable. Many schools see going hybrid as an opportunity to cut teaching costs by dramatically raising the student: faculty ratio. We do not advocate raising the ratio or cutting faculty positions. Raising the student: faculty ratio risks destroying the thing that makes higher education so impactful: personal interaction (Matson and Clark, 2020). Moreover, teaching is a relatively small part of the cost of higher education (based on an analysis we commissioned in 2017, teaching is about 20% of most university budgets) (Katzman, 2017).

The right way to lower the cost of higher ed while creating an environment where online learners will thrive is to address the other 80% of costs. *Hybrid* courses demand an *agile* university.

The Agile Organization

The first wave of online higher education – an ongoing wave --has been siloed, as has the first wave of online companies. This once made sense—it's easiest to protect something small and innovative by distancing it from people's everyday work. But it had a cost; that separation added new complexity with a redundant set of support, placement, technology, marketing, and recruiting efforts and a clunky set of structures for students wanting to move between online and on-campus modalities. Now that online is an important part of higher education, the right structures should be responsive, efficient, and integrated, able to support students and faculty regardless of modality. The growth of enrollment allowed by online and hybrid programs creates an opportunity to build those structures and transition staff to the new structures over time.

The word "agile" has specific connotations in the tech world today, but here we are referring simply to its dictionary definition: "able to move quickly and easily." Originally, most organizations handled taking their services online as a separate venture with a separate team and, in many cases, separate investors (e.g., Verizon and Verizon Wireless). But all of them have increasingly blended their approaches. For example, Home Depot does not care if people buy a hammer at the store or buy it online or if they want to pick it up in-store or have it delivered. The systems are fully integrated, data-driven, and efficient, in other words – agile. At an agile university, we assert that support services should be similarly integrated, and students should have the ability to move quickly and easily between online and in-person learning. Students' schedules and personal preferences should dictate the nature of that movement, but the quality of the learning experience should remain consistent throughout. Online students' access to campus resources, services, and events should be uninhibited, as if they were on campus.

Scale

Increasing enrollment by scaling through high-quality online courses can help defray the cost of creating those courses. As noted, building a good online course is expensive. We generally ask for 150 hours of a professor's time and spend $60,000 on learning design and rich media, plus $15,000 per year after that to update it. And we've seen schools spend many times that.

With no increase in student enrollment, these costs would be unsustainable for many schools. Yet building courses less expensively can be even more problematic, as it leaves institutions facing competitors whose courses are better thought-through and better presented. By adding 50-100 students a year into a course, that expense is borne by $100,000-500,000 per year in tuition for that course, making the spending far less onerous.

Of course, the scale has its own calculus. If an institution accepts online students who are less qualified than its current students, it will lose the trust of its faculty, alumni, and campus-based students. Growing requires sufficient marketing to attract qualified students in numbers large enough to defray content and teaching costs. Scale with integrity generally translates to better reputations…and rankings (the correlation between the enrollments of the top 60 US business schools and their *US News* rankings is 0.79–our own calculation using public *US News* data).

One ecosystem

The agile campus consists of one learning ecosystem, accessible and fluid, such that all resources, events, and courses are accessible to campus members regardless of their location. Rather than duplicate processes and services from the on-ground program for the online program, there is one program, one set of services, and one technology platform. The support that faculty and students need to succeed in this environment is available intuitively, in various modalities, and in anticipation of need.

The agile environment is outcomes-driven, adapts to each learner's needs, provides a real-time performance assessment, and supports collaborative learning. The agile environment does this by creating a social learning environment that connects online and on-campus students. The end result is an ecosystem that creates a powerful experience for all campus community members. It is important to stress the importance of the unified system: using a hybrid strategy does not make a university agile. It's the other way around; streamlining systems intelligently will facilitate hybrid and online instruction.

External Resources

The idea that everything must be done in-house has long been abandoned by any organization seeking efficiency and effectiveness, and many campuses have outsourced some services (food service, bookstores, even residential facility management) successfully. To paraphrase Lankford and Parsa (1999), outsourcing (or partnering with external providers) many support areas allows an institution to focus on its core functions – teaching, research, and service.

Outsourcing is tougher than it looks; to be successful, it requires collaboration between organizational cultures. Higher education's governance structure, mission, and institutional culture can be practically and perceptually at odds with those of its outsourcing partners, often for-profit companies organized around hierarchical decision-making and 70% gross profit margins. Further, making those partnerships successful can require greater management than some institutions anticipated or resourced. Finding the right partners and devoting sufficient resources to support and monitor those providers is an important exercise and must be factored into the cost model.

Collaboration at Scale

The network is the solution. The more campus departments collaborate on services and resources, the more affordable the hybrid, agile campus becomes. Better yet, campuses that embrace the many opportunities to collaborate across institutions in ways that do not commoditize them or threaten their competitive advantage achieve even greater quality and savings.

How would this work? One example takes a page from faculty creation of textbooks that are adopted by many different programs and universities without diminishing the competitive edge of the author or the author's home campus. Some of the "assets" created to support learning in asynchronous ways – a simulation or a case study, for example – could be licensed to other institutions and instructors for use in their courses. The leasing allows the originators to recover some or all of the cost of creating the asset while giving access to programs that could not otherwise have afforded to create it themselves (allowing access to just three non-competitive programs cuts the cost of the content by 75% – University A creates a $20k asset. Three other non-competitive schools are using it, each paying University A $5k, lower cost by 75% without making the experience generic).

What makes a program unique and excellent is rarely an asset it uses, such as a case, but almost always the quality of instruction – what the faculty do with that case – and the student body itself. Just as using the same textbook does not diminish the perceived value of one program over another, neither does leasing course assets. But that collaboration can stimulate a more creative learning experience and better outcomes for the students, depending on how that asset is integrated into the experience.

Agile by Functional Area

Agility should not be limited to courses. Each functional area of a campus needs to adapt.

Student Services. As noted, the units and tools supporting student success should work seamlessly across modalities. Students in a given program, whether it is online, on-campus, or both, need one person with a reasonable caseload who is watching out for them, monitoring success analytics to anticipate students' needs, connecting them to resources, and demonstrating that the institution is invested in their success. A single advisor seeing the student all the way through, regardless of modality, asks, "Is this student on track to a good outcome?"

Online students require this "one-stop-shop" structure because if they are not on campus, navigating the university's infrastructure can pose a sizable barrier to their success. A good coach with a bounded number of students, great tools that suggest who is thriving or struggling, and the mandate to champion the students' problems is profoundly important to the success of online programs and is great for on-campus students as well–and for the institutions themselves. Ultimately, the hybrid program includes and involves the entire campus community and the distinction between online and on-ground dissolves.

Consider the advent of the 311 helpline. First used in Baltimore in 1996, it replaced such things as the "blue pages" in NYC, which had a hundred pages of services in its phone book, with a single number staffed by people who could route the request to the problem-solvers. While it represented good customer service, it was really about gathering information and tracking needs. Through the activity of the 311 system, the city learned details about types, frequencies, and locations of problems, and learned the patterns of departments' performance. It was able to redeploy resources to align with those patterns. Institutions can design systems and prioritize and redirect resources more effectively once they have the data to track students' needs and usage. Their teams will be in a position actually to improve infrastructure and make it more efficient. These improvements are not just good for online programs; they are just good for traditional on-ground programs.

Academic Technology. Hybrid and online tech needs are a superset of traditional on-campus programs. Learning Management Systems (LMSs) have long been used by most professors as places to post syllabi and assignments; in an online or hybrid environment, they have to be prepared to replace the campus itself, facilitating the social interactions that define traditional higher ed. Those interactions happen in the classroom, in the form of rich discussion and collaboration, but outside it as well.

The lack of social functionality in virtually every campus academic platform is not an isolated problem; at each of 4500 US colleges and universities, a small group is charged with evaluating, stitching together, and supporting a wide range of technologies to address a disparate set of needs across campus. The result is 4500 terrible user experiences for both students and faculties. While more easily tolerated by on-campus students, an agile approach (and perhaps a more collaborative one, since no university differentiates itself by the quality of its academic tech stack) would yield a richer dialogue and a tighter community for everyone while making it less jarring when a professor or student decided to teach or take a course online.

Learning Design. Moving programs online has exposed two truths: (a) we should be designing all programs for "online first," and (b) many academic programs could benefit from a thorough refresh process. Let's look at each of these assertions.

Online first. When app designers begin, they start with the mobile version of the application first. They do this because the mobile environment is smaller and more limiting compared to the desktop, and more people access information through their phones than on a desktop or laptop. When they transfer the same application to a desktop, they can expand functionality, but first, they must get the most critical components working for mobile phones.

The same process should be true for the design of courses. We should be designing for asynchronous online first because, like mobile phones, it is a more limiting environment in some ways than a face-to-face or hybrid classroom and because more and more people will expect to access higher education online. Once the learning experience has been architected for the online space, it can be modified or expanded upon for the hybrid or purely on-campus experience. And starting with online first encourages faculty to think about how they will use those resources if and when they teach on campus.

Engage in a program refresh before going online. Faculty do not often have a chance to review an academic program as a whole. They constantly revise or tweak their own courses, but conversations reflecting on the performance of an entire program are rare. Certainly, re-accreditation processes expect such an examination, but those happen on average about every seven years. If an institution is going to invest in creating a hybrid program, taking the time to interrogate the program can lead to even better learning experiences. What kinds of things should be asked? We suggest that program faculty consider the outcomes they expect once students graduate – what should the program be known for, and where are those things taught in the curriculum? What content and experiences tie the courses to the program, the program to the school, and the school to the institution? Next, what among the key knowledge and skills is best learned in real-time? What is best-learned face-to-face (but not necessarily on campus), and what must be learned while on campus? Everything else can be developed as engaging, asynchronous learning experiences.

To create those experiences, we encourage program designers to look for opportunities to maximize students' engagement with the content, peers, faculty, and staff. Much of the online content we have seen looks too much like an ebook – a one-way push of predominantly text-based information. Instead, we should be asking: Where does it make sense to expose students to real-time problems using interactive case studies, or to provide multiple opportunities to practice using short simulations, or collaborate with peers using collaborative annotation tools, or engage in authentic assessments aligned to the type of knowledge being learned? It can be worth investing in designing these kinds of learning opportunities, particularly when they can also be used for similar courses that meet on campus or when the knowledge or skill spans multiple disciplines, such as statistics or coding.

Marketing. Most online students go to schools within 50 miles of campus (Noodle largely works with schools with national reputations, but even for us, most students come from within 200 miles). That means a program generally competes for online and hybrid students on three axes: discipline, prestige, and geography. In other words, the Tufts Public Health program does not compete for students with the university's own engineering school, UMass/Boston's public health program, or Texas A&M's public health program (which shares its *US News* ranking).

If a program cannot market effectively within its niche, the increased capacity of its competitors will push it to a lower tier of prestige because it cannot change geography or discipline. As online programs continue to grow at the expense of on-campus programs, marketing for each, then, will continue to grow in cost and importance. An agile approach to marketing will best help it keep costs under control while protecting its catchment.

Multiple starts. Agile online programs tend to have specific and multiple start dates; they do not start only every August. Students seeking online programs expect that flexibility – that when they are ready to start, they can. If the first day of class is more than three months from the time the prospective student indicates interest in a program, that prospective student will probably not enroll in that program because they will find a comparable program that is available now. They are not unreasonable; how long are you willing to wait for a table at a restaurant if you know an equally good restaurant nearby can take you now? We are not saying that programs need to begin every week – starting three times a year can satisfy most eager students. In higher education, very few programs are so good that students will wait months and months to enroll.

Outreach. Even for a program "that good," it is important to be responsive when a student expresses an interest: calling and emailing them are table stakes in the online world. Noodle occasionally does experiments asking what happens if we don't call a prospective student who has indicated an interest in a top-tier school, and the result is an overwhelming drop in enrollment. It is odd that some universities think it is beneath them to cultivate prospective students, answer their questions, and help them figure out whether they are a good fit; most organizations offering expensive goods and services, like Tiffany's or Tesla, treat prospects in welcoming ways. To achieve the scale needed to support great online or hybrid learning, outreach needs to become part of the marketing strategy. And since a great majority of prospective and current student contacts from hybrid programs come in outside traditional business hours, the counseling teams must be flexible.

It's noteworthy that some campuses still use two completely different recruiting models, one for on-campus and one for online prospects. This bifurcation creates enormous barriers for both the staff and prospective students. Particularly concerning is when the incentives for recruiting for two versions of the same program differ because each team has an incentive to sell the student its version of the program, not what's best for the student. Some schools address this problem by stopping the online team from marketing within 50 miles of campus; this simply hands nearby prospects to online universities willing to talk with them. Better is to create one infrastructure supporting programs of all modalities, with unified recruiting goals and a focus on what is best for the student.

Keyword strategies. Institutions first started recruiting for online programs the way they did for on-ground, where traditionally, they spent 1-2 percent of tuition on marketing and recruiting. Online programs require a much more strategic digital strategy. Many students use Google to find a program; where an institution appears on a search page matters as much as its *US News* ranking. As more programs compete for the same keywords, they become more expensive; an institution can easily spend hundreds of dollars per click on someone interested in a program. Many institutions are spending 30-40 percent of tuition on marketing, which is a problem (Newton, 2016).

Why a Coherent Ecosystem Matters

For the wealthiest and most in-demand schools, it doesn't.

For everyone else, a synthetic approach to systems, services, teaching, and technology will create more resilient, scalable, and responsive universities, both for degree programs and lifelong learning. Great hybrid learning will be right at home at these schools; moreover, they will be able to lower tuition while reinvesting in continual improvement.

A hybrid approach has the potential to improve universities significantly, more so if it's part of an agile approach. Supercharged by

COVID, the move to online education has been exceptionally fast by higher ed standards. This is the moment to steer the change to something we can all be proud of.

References

Matson, T., and Clark, J. (2020). Improve student outcomes by building caring faculty relationships. Retrieved from: https://www.gallup.com/education/286514/improve-student-outcomes-building-caring-faculty-relationships.aspx

Katzman, J. (2017). It came easy: Revenue and cost drivers in higher ed and their implications. Unpublished manuscript.

Lankford, W.M. and Parsa, F. (1999). Outsourcing: a primer. *Management Decision*, 37(4), pp. 310-316. Retrieved from: https://doi.org/10.1108/00251749910269357

Newton, D. (2016). The $100 billion higher ed arms race no one can afford. *Huffington Post,* Dec 14. Retrieved from: https://www.huffpost.com/entry/the-100-billion-higher-ed-arms-race-no-one-can-afford_b_58515d24e4b0a464fad3e565.

Walton Family Foundation. (2020). *Opening Doors to Opportunity: Generation Z and Millennials Speak.* Retrieved from: https://8ce82b94a8c4fdc3ea6d-b1d233e3bc3cb10858bea65ff05e18f2.ssl.cf2.rackcdn.com/b1/02/ddcbc1d6434d91e8494f0070fa96/echelon-insights-walton-family-foundation-generation-z-millennials-and-opportunity-report-october-2020-10-6-20.pdf

Chapter 5

David P. Green

Ensuring Success when Developing Hybrid Learning Interventions

Abstract

Implementing well-designed hybrid learning interventions requires a significant investment of an educator's time and effort. While experts in their professional domains, educators might lack the fundamental knowledge and skills needed with hybrid course design best practices, which might influence their willingness to innovate with their classes. A self-evaluation checklist is presented alongside multiple resources that help individual faculty members identify individualized and targeted professional development strategies when implementing hybrid learning interventions. Knowledge, motivation, and organizational influences all contribute to the circumstances under which an educator is operating during hybrid course redesigns and inform their professional development choices. This chapter should be applicable to trainers and educators who are guiding complex educational reform initiatives.

Introduction

Amidst rigid traditionalism and with a fundamental lack of relevant knowledge and skills, how do faculty members successfully create innovative, high-quality hybrid courses? In an area where faculty members are subject matter experts but are generally novices in hybrid course design, they often rely on expertise from learning design teams. However, the mismatch between education's traditional hierarchical structure and the need for curricular innovation by faculty members yields creative tension (Senge, 1990). In this chapter, we consider how to help faculty members develop the expertise necessary to develop innovative, hybrid courses.

Educators are not isolated individuals but instead operate within social, professional environments where interactions, discourses, and ideologies shape their social and creative identities and influence their innovative engagements (Glaveanu & Tanggaard, 2014). Thus, individual educators may approach discussions about developing hybrid learning environments through a wide range of perspectives. Their participation in conversations and perspectives on assumed needs will be shaped largely by how they view their own level of comfort with being creative as an educator amidst their social and professional environments. As a result, knowledge, motivation, and organizational needs are likely to be impacted by an educator's own enthusiasm to innovate.

Willingness to Innovate with Hybrid Learning

The willingness to innovate is aligned with high motivation and the ability to be a self-directed learner. An individual could have all the knowledge needed to be creative yet lack the motivation to get started, so they will never make the choice to begin. On the other hand, a creative educator might have all the intrinsic motivation to get started, may or may not have the knowledge, but can increase knowledge over time because they are a self-directed learner. Therefore, when educators wish to develop hybrid education interventions, they must try to align their choices of professional development strategies with this in mind. One way to accomplish this alignment is to perform a self-evaluation related to one's own knowledge and motivation needs. As mentioned previously, educators approach innovation with different levels of comfort. This willingness (or lack of willingness) to innovate can be self-measured using the checklist provided in Table 1 and ideally occurs at the outset of a new hybrid course redesign effort. After self-evaluating one's own willingness to innovate by developing hybrid learning experiences, this information can be used to inform future choices on how to identify appropriate and meaningful professional development opportunities.

Table 5.1 Self-evaluation checklist for faculty members

	Ask yourself, which of these seems most like me?	Then I should seek professional development that helps me to:
☐	I need direction in implementing hybrid learning within my classes.	• increase my factual, conceptual, procedural, and metacognitive knowledge. • incorporate strategies to boost my motivation (intrinsic and extrinsic). • make an active choice to get started.
☐	I have knowledge about hybrid learning design but need motivation.	• incorporate strategies to increase my motivation (intrinsic and extrinsic). • make an active choice to get started.
☐	I am motivated to implement hybrid learning within my classes, but I need guidance.	• increase my factual, conceptual, procedural, and metacognitive knowledge. • incorporate strategies to persist and sustain my motivation (intrinsic and extrinsic).
☐	I have appropriate levels of knowledge and ample motivation to get started with implementing hybrid learning within my classes.	• feel empowered to demonstrate my factual, conceptual, procedural, and metacognitive knowledge
☐	I have high levels of knowledge and high motivation to get started with implementing hybrid learning within my classes.	• serve as an "educator-champion" who should be trusted to innovate effectively. • stimulate my colleagues by sharing my success stories.

Key Professional Development Considerations When Designing a Hybrid Classroom

Educators who strive to effectively lead exceptional hybrid learning environments will likely seek out specialized professional development to craft meaningful educational experiences for their learners. In addition to learning design and development assistance, educators will look for fundamental sources of organizational support. Therefore, educators should align their unique needs with targeted professional development and organizational support offerings.

Effective hybrid learning experiences incorporate sound learning design that is based on educational best practices. And given the variety of circumstances and intricacies that comprise the hybrid "classroom," an educator has myriad factors to consider and master (in addition to the academic content itself). Identifying fundamental knowledge and skills needed to develop hybrid learning experiences might provide additional insight into where an educator should focus their energy when participating in professional development opportunities (Table 5.2).

Table 5.2 Fundamental knowledge/skills and focal points for professional development initiatives

Fundamental knowledge and skills	Focal points for professional development
User-friendliness and Inclusivity	accessibility
	language within course artifacts
	reaching every learner
	instinctive course delivery
Alignment	backwards course design
	scaffolding of information, topics, and skills
Learner engagement	cognitive
	behavioral
	affective
Instructor presence	asynchronous activities and tasks within LMS
	synchronous sessions (online classroom space)
	synchronous sessions (physical classroom space)
Interaction	with content: active practice, targeted/formative feedback, and critical reflection
	with classmates: asynchronous peer-to-peer learning within LMS
	with classmates: synchronous peer-to-peer learning within physical and digital classroom spaces
	with course director: instructor-learner
Relevance	connecting academic content with learners' daily lives
	why the content matters to learners
	authentic assessments
Clarity	course expectations
	learning path
	instructions
	overall course organization
Variety	delivery of information
	tasks
	information
	teaching strategies
	assessment approaches (formative)
	assessment approaches (summative)
Technology	learning management system (LMS)
	digital classroom spaces
	physical classroom space (audio-visual)

After self-evaluating one's own willingness to innovate by designing hybrid learning interventions and identifying which fundamental knowledge and skills need to be gained or developed, an educator can begin to identify what kinds of professional development opportunities suit their unique knowledge and motivation needs. Today's educators have access to many professional development opportunities. Depending on their own professional organizations, they may have opportunities provided for them. In other cases, they might need to seek out online information or online communities to join. Table 5.3 provides a summary of potential professional development opportunities with anticipated outcomes that are available.

Table 5.3 Professional development opportunities for educators

Opportunity	Description	Anticipated Outcomes
Online courses or workshops	Take online courses or workshops from reputable organizations and educational institutions to learn about hybrid learning.	Improved understanding of hybrid learning and best practices, ability to design and implement effective hybrid learning experiences
Conferences or webinars	Attend conferences or webinars to learn from experts in the field and stay informed of the latest developments.	Improved knowledge of current trends and best practices in hybrid learning, exposure to new ideas and innovative approaches
Networking	Join online groups or forums to connect with other professionals and exchange ideas.	Increased professional connections, exposure to new ideas and approaches, opportunity to collaborate and share experiences
Collaboration	Partner with other faculty members or educational institutions to share resources, ideas, and experiences.	Improved teaching methods through collaboration and sharing of experiences, access to a wider range of resources and ideas
Self-reflection and experimentation	Experiment with different approaches to hybrid learning and reflect on your experiences to continuously improve your teaching methods.	Improved teaching methods through self-reflection and experimentation, ability to effectively adapt to changing needs and demands of students
Professional Learning Communities (PLCs)	Join or create a PLC with colleagues to collaborate and share experiences.	Improved teaching methods through collaboration and sharing of experiences, increased opportunities for professional growth and development
Books and articles	Read books and academic articles to learn about best practices and current trends.	Improved knowledge of best practices and current trends in hybrid learning, ability to stay informed of the latest developments and innovations
On-campus workshops or training sessions	Attend in-person workshops or training sessions offered by your	Improved understanding of hybrid learning and best practices, ability to design and

	institution or professional organizations.	implement effective hybrid learning experiences
Virtual or augmented reality experiences	Explore the use of virtual or augmented reality in the classroom to enhance the hybrid learning experience.	Improved understanding of the use of virtual or augmented reality in hybrid learning, ability to effectively incorporate technology into hybrid learning experiences
Observing best practices in other schools	Visit other schools that have successfully implemented hybrid learning to learn from their experiences and best practices.	Improved understanding of best practices and successful approaches in hybrid learning, exposure to new ideas and innovative approaches
Instructional design courses or certifications	Take courses or obtain certifications in instructional design to understand how to design effective hybrid learning experiences.	Improved understanding of instructional design principles and best practices, ability to design effective hybrid learning experiences
Online teacher communities	Join online communities to share resources and connect with other teachers and educators.	Increased professional connections, exposure to new ideas and approaches, opportunity to collaborate and share experiences
Incorporating technology tools and resources	Explore the use of technology tools and resources to enhance the hybrid learning experience.	Improved use of technology in hybrid learning, increased student engagement and motivation, ability to effectively incorporate technology into hybrid learning experiences
Participating in research studies	Participate in research studies to contribute to the field and stay informed of the latest developments and trends.	Improved knowledge of current research and trends in hybrid learning, the opportunity to contribute to the field and make a positive impact
Staying current with emerging technologies	Stay informed of emerging technologies and innovations in hybrid learning.	Improved knowledge of emerging technologies and innovations, ability to effectively incorporate new technologies into hybrid learning experiences

Proposed Action Plan for Improved Accountability Practices

Accountability mechanisms are also part of the social culture in which educators operate. The organization-educator relationship is complex, but return-on-investment of professional development activities is important for stakeholders to consider. For example, significant financial resources, human capital, and technology are usually required to implement quality initiatives. Thus, an action plan with embedded strategies is proposed to improve accountability practices (Table 5.4).

Table 5.4 Action plan strategies mapped to the nested accountability levels

Level	Mission / Goal	Strategy
Organizational	Organizational Priorities from Strategic Plan	Relate accountability practices to Institutional-level Educational Objectives (ILEOs)
Departmental	Organizational goal	Relate accountability practices to expected best practices for hybrid course designs
Instructor	Stakeholder key results	Relate accountability practices to student outcomes

At the organizational level, accountability practices need to be related to existing institutional-level educational objectives (ILEOs). At the departmental level, accountability practices should relate to existing best practices for hybrid course design. At the individual level, accountability practices should relate to student performance outcomes. Aligning values amongst all stakeholders during hybrid course design initiatives will likely yield improved accountability with concrete decision rights and superior learning environments for students.

Ensuring Success with Hybrid Learning Interventions: Diagnostic Benchmarking

Organizations frequently compare performance, processes, and practices against their peer institutions to scrutinize internal successes and identify opportunities for growth (Bender & Schuh, 2002; Dowd, 2005). These strategic benchmarking processes are used to evaluate whether or not organizational goals are being met (Bender & Schuh,

2002). Peer-based benchmarking requires that organizations use similar comparison institutions in terms of values, best practices, and educational criteria (Dowd, 2005). Ultimately, hybrid educational initiatives incorporate diagnostic peer-based benchmarking processes to align stakeholder values and approaches to maximize learner performance (Doerfel & Ruben, 2002; Dowd, 2005).

Table 5.5 proposes seven performance metrics, the associated goal for each performance metric analysis, and a brief synopsis of what can be gleaned from a gap analysis. Collectively, the performance metrics will yield information related to effort over time, faculty demographics, student demographics, diversity, equity of resources, student academic performance, organizational resources committed to technology support, professional development support, financial accountability, and contributions toward faculty scholarship. Following the analysis of these metrics, educators should be able to detect the root causes of any performance issues by analyzing performance gaps. Such a gap analysis would yield information about knowledge issues that limit successful hybrid course redesigns, motivational factors that limit participation in hybrid projects, and organizational limitations that diminish the likelihood of successful projects (Table 5.5).

Table 5.5 Performance metrics to be used in peer-based benchmarking process aligned with corresponding goals and how this relates to a KMO gap analysis

Performance Metrics	Goals	Gap Analysis
# of hybrid education interventions redesigned over time	• To compare the trajectory of hybrid course redesign projects with peer institutions.	When performance metrics are compared with similar metrics from peer institutions, educators should be able to identify the root causes of the performance issue by analyzing relevant performance gaps:

• Knowledge issues that limit hybrid course redesigns;
• Motivational factors that limit participation in hybrid course redesign projects; |
| # of faculty participating in innovative hybrid education reform projects over time and faculty demographic information | • To evaluate the success or failure of faculty participation.
• To evaluate the diversity of faculty members who participate. | |

Cumulative hours of training sessions and faculty development seminars conducted Fiscal resources allocated toward technology support per faculty effort	• To compare demonstrated organizational effort to enhance faculty knowledge, skills, and motivation. • To examine institutional financial support and accountability mechanisms.	• Organizational limitations that diminish the likelihood of successful implementation of hybrid learning intervention projects.
Student performance and demographic metrics % of student tuition/fees that support hybrid teaching and technology needs	• To directly assess the impact of hybrid classrooms on student learning, both within and across institutions. • To determine the equity of resources and potential influences on educational outcomes.	
# of peer-reviewed publications resulting from innovative hybrid course redesigns	• To review the impact faculty effort has on scholarship.	

Knowledge, motivation, and organizational gaps (KMO) are influences that contribute to an increased faculty hesitancy in creating hybrid classrooms. For example, faculty members might currently lack knowledge of best practices for hybrid course designs and pedagogy. Also, skills development is likely needed with educational technologies and learning management systems. Additionally, motivational influences are likely present when teaching activities are not tied directly to promotion. Intrinsic motivation might also be lacking when students generally do well academically already, so faculty members see little need to modify their teaching strategies. However, improvements can be made with organizational influences. When initiatives are relatively new, many faculty members are unaware that support exists for their academic technology needs. Finally, internal politics can be an influence because some faculty members see learning design teams as their "replacer" rather than a partner for assistance.

The proposed strategic benchmarking process with associated performance metrics just described accounts for effort, diversity, equity, resource allocation, financial accountability, and stakeholder performance. Data-driven and evidence-based benchmarking approaches enhance accountability systems (Marsh, 2012; Marsh & Farrell, 2015). Dowd (2005) defined diagnostic benchmarking as a "health check" to help identify opportunities for performance growth (p. 7). Innovative initiatives, like the implementation of hybrid learning interventions, can compare performance metrics and evaluate performance issues. This relevant diagnostic benchmarking analysis of appropriate performance metrics could be the "health check" needed to ensure success with hybrid learning initiatives (Dowd, 2005, p. 7).

Conclusion

The self-evaluation checklist for targeted professional development aligns knowledge and motivation dimensions with individual educator needs over time. Specialized professional development initiatives to support educators who are developing hybrid learning interventions require significant organizational contributions (fiscal, human capital, and technology). Therefore, an extension of the social intersections for educators within their professional environments are accountability relationships. Adequate return on investment for costly professional development initiatives must be ensured. However, the traditionalism of education's hierarchical structure makes accountability processes challenging and can limit the effectiveness of novel initiatives. Therefore, the action plan for improving misaligned professional accountability relationships fosters a data-driven culture change built upon shared values by incorporating a sound, evidence-based diagnostic benchmarking strategy (Dowd, 2005; Marsh, 2012; Marsh & Farrell, 2015). If novel hybrid classroom initiatives are to succeed and answer the call to action for educational reform, then self-motivated faculty members who are empowered to innovate will fuel organization-wide performance gains.

References

Bender, B.E. and Schuh, J.H. (2002), Editors' notes. *New Directions for Higher Education*, Vol. 118, pp. 1–4. doi: 10.1002/he.52

Bronfenbrenner, U. (1979). *The ecology of human development: Experiments by nature and design.* Cambridge, Mass: Harvard University Press.

Caiazza, R., & Simoni, M. (2015). Directors' role in inter-organizational networks. *Corporate Governance, 15*(4), 508-516. doi:10.1108/CG-05-2014-0059

Caiazza, R., Cannella Jr, A. A., Phan, P. H., & Simoni, M. (2019). An institutional contingency perspective of interlocking directorates. *International Journal of Management Reviews, 21*(3), 277-293. doi:10.1111/ijmr.12182

Carte, T. A., Chidambaram, L., & Becker, A. (2006). Emergent leadership in self-managed virtual teams: A longitudinal study of concentrated and shared leadership behaviors. *Group Decision and Negotiation, 15*(4), 323-343. doi:10.1007/s10726-006-9045-7

Courpasson, D., Dany, F., & Clegg, S. (2012). Resisters at work: Generating productive resistance in the workplace. *Organization Science, 23*(3), 801-819. doi:10.1287/orsc.1110.0657

Doerfel, M.L. and Ruben, B.D. (2002), Developing more adaptive, innovative, and interactive organizations. *New Directions for Higher Education*, Vol. 118, pp. 5-28. doi:10.1002/he.53

Dowd, A.C. (2005), *Data don't drive: Building a practitioner-driven culture of inquiry to assess community college performance.* Boston: University of Massachusetts, Lumina Foundation for Education. Retrieved from https://files.eric.ed.gov/fulltext/ED499777.pdf

Dubnick, M.J. (2003), Accountability and ethics: Reconsidering the relationships. *International Journal of Organization Theory and*

Behavior, Vol. 6 No. 3, pp. 405–441. Retrieved from http://libproxy.usc.edu/login?url=http://search.proquest.com.libproxy2.usc.edu/docview/212039270?accountid=14749

Elmore, R.F. (2002), *Bridging the gap between standards and achievement.* Report, Washington, DC: Albert Shanker Institute. Retrieved July 12, 2003, from http://www.shankerinstitute.org/resource/bridging-gap-between-standards-and-achievement

Erez, M., & Gati, E. (2004), A dynamic, multi-level model of culture: from the micro level of the individual to the macro level of a global culture. *Applied Psychology*, 53, 583–598. doi:10.1111/j.1464-0597.2004.00190.x

Green, D.P. (2016), Next generation medical education: facilitating student-centered learning environments. *Educause ELI Briefs*, Vol. 2016, pp. 1-6. Retrieved from https://library.educause.edu/resources/2016/3/next-generation-medical-education

Green, D.P. (2018), A gap analysis of course directors' effective implementation of technology-enriched course designs: An innovation study. Doctoral Dissertation, University of Southern California Rossier School of Education, USA.

Green, D.P. (2019), Foundational elements of school-specific augmented medical education. *Medical Science Educator*, Vol. 29 No. 2, pp. 561-569. doi: 10.1007/s40670-019-00702-8

Hempel, P. S., Zhang, Z., & Han, Y. (2012), Team empowerment and the organizational context: Decentralization and the contrasting effects of formalization. *Journal of Management, 38*(2), 475-501. doi:10.1177/0149206309342891

Hentschke, G.C. and Wohlstetter, P. (2004), Cracking the code of accountability. *University of Southern California Urban Education*, Spring/Summer, pp. 17–19.

Hurtubise, L., Hall, E., Sheridan, L., and Han, H. (2015), The flipped classroom in medical education: Engaging students to build competency. *Journal of Medical Education and Curricular Development*, Vol. 2, pp. 235-43. doi:10.4137/JMECD.S23895

LCME. (2016), Liaison Committee on Medical Education About. Available at: http://lcme.org/about/

Lipton, M. (1996), Demystifying the development of an organizational vision. *Sloan Management Review, Vol. 37 No. 4*, pp. 83–92.

Marsh, J.A. (2012), Interventions promoting educators' use of data: Research insights and gaps. *Teachers College Record*, Vol. 114 No. 11, pp. 1-48.

Marsh, J.A. and Farrell, C.C. (2015), How leaders can support teachers with data-driven decision making: A framework for understanding capacity building. *Educational Management Administration & Leadership*, Vol. 43 No. 2, pp. 269-289. doi:10.1177/1741143214537229

McDonald, R. (2007), An investigation of innovation in non-profit organizations: The role of organizational mission. *Nonprofit and Voluntary Sector Quarterly, Vol. 36* No. 2, pp. 256–281. doi:10.1177/0899764006295996

Mehta, N.B., Hull, A.L., Young, J.B., and Stoller, J.K. (2013), Just imagine: New paradigms for medical education. *Academic Medicine*, Vol. 88 No. 10, pp. 1418-1423. doi:10.1097/ACM.0b013e3182a36a07

Pincus, J. (2006), Communication satisfaction, job satisfaction and job performance. *Human Communications Research, Vol. 12* No. 2, pp. 395–419.

Prober, C.G. and Heath, C. (2012), Lecture halls without lectures—a proposal for medical education. *The New England Journal of Medicine*, Vol. 366 No. 18, pp. 1657-1659. doi:10.1056/NEJMp1202451

Prober, C.G. and Khan, S. (2013), Medical education reimagined: A call to action. *Academic Medicine*, Vol. 88 No. 10, pp. 1407-1410. doi:10.1097/ACM.0b013e3182a368bd

Romme, A. G. L. (2019). Climbing up and down the hierarchy of accountability: Implications for organization design. *Journal of Organization Design, 8*(1), 1-14. doi:10.1186/s41469-019-0060-y

Romzek, B.S. and Dubnick, M.J. (1987), Accountability in the public sector: Lessons from the Challenger tragedy. *Public Administration Review*, Vol. 47 No. 3, pp. 227-238.

Schein, E. (2004), "How leaders embed and transmit culture", in Schein, E. (Ed.), *Organizational culture and leadership* (3rd ed,), Jossey-Bass, San Francisco, CA, pp. 245–271.

Senge, P. (1990), The leader's new work: Building learning organizations. *Sloan Management Review, Vol. 32* No. 1, pp. 7–22.

HELLO Initiative. (2016), HELLO Initiative Welcome. Available at: website removed for anonymity

USM. (2016), Urban School of Medicine MD Program Curriculum. Available at: website removed for anonymity

Wang, D., Waldman, D. A., & Ashforth, B. E. (2019). Building relationships through accountability: An expanded idea of accountability. *Organizational Psychology Review, 9*(2-3), 184-206. doi:10.1177/2041386619878876

Chapter 6

Aaron Rasmussen and Kristen Przyborski

Subdividing Synchrony: Finding Opportunities for Meaningful Interaction in Online Courses

Abstract

The most valuable and scarcest resource in education is synchronous teaching performed by a human. Hybrid learning provides the unique opportunity to maximize the effectiveness of time and capital spent on this type of teaching. The question becomes: How do you choose how to spend a human teacher's synchronous time? This chapter provides an overview of best practices in selecting which aspects of a course should be instructor-synchronous, peer-synchronous one-to-one, peer-synchronous one-to-many, AI-synchronous, asynchronous, and the associated tools.

Introduction

The scarcest and most valuable resource in education is one-to-one, synchronous instruction between a teacher—an expert who has devoted significant time to learning and teaching a particular discipline—and a student. Opportunities for interaction between students and teachers and also between students are important for learning and engagement. These opportunities are difficult to orchestrate due to limited time and knowledge of and access to pedagogical tools. These problems are exacerbated in online environments. At Outlier.org, where we make for-credit and scalable online college courses, we've spent a long time thinking about how best to effectively and efficiently facilitate meaningful interactions between teacher and student and, additionally, improve the quality of other interactions, like peer-to-peer. By improving the efficiency of online course creation, instructors have more time to instruct, coach, and mentor their students. Additionally, through creative pedagogical design, instructors can facilitate effective interactions between peers, creating further opportunities to build community and connection while promoting clarity.

Efficient and Engaging Asynchronous Instruction

Instructor time is a scarce resource. As with any scarce resource, we should maximize its benefits while doing all we can to preserve it. Asynchronous classes provide an opportunity to maximize instructor time through automation. Asynchronous content delivery is not bound by time and space, which allows students to self-pace their interactions with course materials. Asynchronous communication between an instructor and a student typically takes the form of pre-recorded instructor lessons, email, discussion boards, large media platforms (e.g., TikTok, YouTube), chats, grading, and feedback. In theory, increasing the number of channels available for communication should increase opportunities for instructor-to-student interaction. In reality, the faculty workload in online courses is such that communication between instructor and student occurs mostly through feedback, grading, and discussion board facilitation; that is, in spite of myriad channels of communication, instructors often only use feedback on graded assignments as a method of interaction because there simply isn't time to do more.

Instructor workload for online classes is already higher than for face-to-face courses, but it is also categorized differently (Anderson & Avery, 2008). Creating and organizing online materials and the additional labor that goes into managing the tools necessary to communicate with individual students online means that little time is left for meaningful one-on-one teacher-student interaction, whether asynchronous or synchronous (Cavanaugh, 2005). Instead, instructor time is frequently spent on one-to-many interactions that could be accomplished with the aid of technological tools. The goal of freeing up instructor time has not been realized in many cases because of the massive investment of time and money required to create and integrate new technologies.

Table 6.1 How faculty spend their time in online classes. Data has been summarized (excluding pre-semester prep-time) into the four broad categories defined by Anderson and Avery (2008).

	Cavanaugh (2005)	Anderson & Avery (2008)	Mandernach
Student evaluation	42%	31%	37%
Student interaction	35%	51%	43%
Instructional content	6%	15%	4%
Other	18%	5%	6%

Asynchronous peer-to-peer interactions can be just as time-consuming as those between instructors and students, depending on the technology used. Online courses' primary peer-to-peer communication channel has been the asynchronous, threaded, text-based discussion board (Martin, Kumar, Ritzhaupt & Polly, 2023). This model arose in the 1990s chat-room-dominated internet ecosystem and has monopolized online classroom spaces into the 2020s, although new models are emerging. In the standard model, discussion prompts are posted by the instructor in a dedicated space. Numerous constraints (e.g., word length, number of responses, availability of posts) are put into place to discourage cheating and coerce meaningful interaction among students. This method of communication is intended to be of the peer-to-peer variety, but the primary driver for participation is the connection to grades, which are instructor-driven (Cifuentes & Hughey, 2019). This direct tie to grades limits students' authentic interactions with each other and the content. Asynchronously delivered courses in this manner seem to provide fewer opportunities for connection than synchronously delivered courses.

Models for Prioritizing Student-to-One Interactions

What would it look like if we prioritized meaningful one-to-one interactions—both between students and between instructors and students—when developing instruction and sought tools that would allow such interactions? It is helpful to look at current models of online education more closely so that we can identify those elements that can occur asynchronously and those that we should prioritize for synchronous one-to-one interactions. Learning consists of *content* interactions and *social* interactions. Video, audio, course pages, quizzes, and other asynchronous content elements allow for flexibility and give students time to process information. Social interactions are valuable for establishing connectedness and relevance, gaining insights, and receiving feedback.

Table 6.2 Typical social course elements of synchronous and asynchronous online courses

	Synchronous	Asynchronous
Instructor-to-student	Office hours, meetings	Assignment clarification, email, feedback, office hours, meetings
Peer-to-peer	Group projects and assignments, study groups, recitation sessions, tutoring, coaching, class discussions	Group projects and assignments, tutoring, coaching
Peer-to-many	Project presentations, class discussions	Facilitated discussion boards
Instructor-to-many	Class time	Facilitation, Recorded Lectures, Announcements, Twitch, Twitter

The importance of one-to-one instruction was demonstrated by Benjamin Bloom (1985) in his foundational study on what he called "the two-sigma problem." Bloom showed that students perform at a level that is two standard deviations above their expected performance if they receive one-to-one feedback that is corrective and timely. Ninety percent of tutored students consistently performed in the top 20% of the class when they received such feedback. Much research has been accomplished since Bloom's time, but the one-to-one ratio is still considered ideal. The problem is that providing this level of attention is resource-intensive and, therefore, impractical for most higher education institutions.

Peer-to-Peer Learning

For most instructors, most of the time, one-to-one tutoring for each student is not possible. However, peers can also provide instruction, coaching, and feedback, potentially improving the performance of all students. Given that students are an abundant resource in classrooms, it is sensible to optimize student peer-to-peer interactions to increase overall learning before optimizing a scarce resource. Although the facilitated asynchronous discussion post is the dominant model in online education, there are other ways to encourage peer-peer connections within an online academic setting. Creating meaningful opportunities for communication and collaboration between peers could help fill in the gaps when there isn't time for direct interaction with an instructor.

Peer-to-peer learning, defined as students learning from and with each other, comes in a variety of forms (e.g., discussion, buddy systems, group projects). The effectiveness depends on many factors, including student personality and the structuring of the activity. Effective peer-to-peer interactions also depend on shared knowledge and experiences. Peers can be matched randomly by ability level, knowledge level, and other criteria chosen by the instructor.

Fortnite as Community/Coaching Tool

An example of how mutual knowledge can be brought into a peer-to-peer learning environment is the video game *Fortnite*, one of the most popular video games in the world (ARM, 2019). Fundamentally, the business model of a modern video game depends on the players learning a relatively complex system and deploying that knowledge within the game. This dependence on the players learning the rule system aligns the incentives of teaching with game companies' profits, yielding a high bias toward effective teaching methods. These teaching methods are nearly entirely peer-to-peer.

Fortnite's entry into the field of K-12 education started out as a problem (Marlatt, 2020). The draw of the Fortnite online community meant that students were playing the game in school and demonstrating unhealthy behaviors such as the late-night playing of the game. Googling "How to play fortnight at school" generates over 33,00,000 results and a rich set of videos and written instructions. Schools now routinely use punitive measures to stave off Fortnite's encroachment into academic spaces and have encouraged parents to ban the game in their homes.

The premise of the game is that 100 players are divided into squads of up to 4 players each and are dropped on an island to battle it out and win. The island itself is over 3 square kilometers, and there is a multitude of weapons, items, strategies, and (of course) forts. Player communities are self-organized in that there is no instructor present. Players, many of whom are still in single-digit ages, learn this complex system by having a shared goal: to win. Online gaming "communities of practice" extend a player's experience through discussion and sharing resources with other similarly motivated players (Marlatt, 2020). Frequently, peer players will direct each other to which parts of the map are good, which weapons they should use, and how they should play. These peers become effective instructors and provide corrective, specific, and timely feedback.

The juxtaposition of our students' coerced participation in their academic discussion boards to passionate engagement in their online gaming communities provides an opportunity. What if we flip this problem and instead ask how Fortnite's success in community building can be replicated in our online learning spaces?

Creating Online Communities

Video game vendors build their online communities intentionally, employing a variety of techniques (Ruggles, Wadley & Gibbs, 2005). At its most basic, the shared goal of winning connects peers to each other. We have found, in considering peer-to-peer instruction, whether synchronous or not, a clear shared goal and win state (passing a class, passing a chapter, acing a quiz) can have an immediate effect on the willingness of students to interact and help each other. Some of this peer-to-peer interaction happens on a learning platform, while we have found some of Outlier's students will interact outside the platform, over Reddit, for example.

Early in an online calculus course we at Outlier.org were developing, we attempted video study groups over Zoom, and it was a terrible failure.

Many students would not show up. Those who did often had their video turned off, and few were brave enough to contribute in a meaningful way. We moved those study groups to Slack and had significantly more success, which we attribute to the low social risk of engagement. For example, a student might give a thumbs-up emoji to a TA-created post. That small amount of commitment can be nurtured. A daring first-follower (Uhl-Bien, Riggio, Lowe, & Carsten. , 2014) —and it just takes one—may post about a problem they are having. This question may encourage other students to interact by adding an emoji. When a peer answers their classmates' questions, the post receives a flurry of thankful emojis from other students. This creates an environment in which there is a social value to answering the questions of one's peers.

We have since transitioned to Yellowdig for this style of communication (see the Chapter in this volume by Roy & Verdine), which is optimized specifically for an academic setting so that instructors can efficiently post prompts and see meaningful analytics on engagement while retaining the low social risk dynamics of Slack. Slack and Yellowdig both provide a more natural emoji-inclusive communication style that our students seem to prefer, but these methods still suffer from the peer-to-many problems we see with traditional discussion boards. Can we encourage students to interact in a more meaningful way with their peers? If so, we may be able to cut back on the heavy emphasis on discussion boards and free up the time instructors must dedicate to their facilitation. We are currently experimenting with a real-time spatial audio meeting place that uses cute avatars instead of Zoom video, as well as a more natural allowance for multiple simultaneous conversations for a less intimidating real-time interaction. This platform is being developed by our VP of Engineering and emulates a format that many students are familiar with using on the online gaming platform Discord.

Subdividing Synchrony

New technologies are promising to make online courses more efficient, freeing up instructor time to interact with students individually.

Some instructional interventions and methodologies are in a nascent stage, while others are more fully matured. These methodologies roughly divide into two categories: Moving synchronous activities like lectures into a high-quality asynchronous delivery format and subdividing the remaining synchronous activities into those that require instructor involvement and those that do not.

For the delivery of lecture material, we at Outlier.org have found success in high-quality cinematic capture of the best instructors delivering their material straight to the camera. Edited for clarity and brevity, these videos have proven to be highly effective teaching tools. Prerecording lectures for later use could save an instructor's valuable time during the term to devote to individual instruction. Although video and editing technologies have a learning curve to use, the value of high-quality recordings lies in increased student engagement and in the reusability of the lecture content.

Automated grading is another way that technology can free up instructor time. With topics such as math, where a math engine can compute equivalencies, and psychology, where multiple-choice tests are common, machine grading asynchronously is effective and, in our experience, predicts future success well—which implies a correct assessment of student learning outcomes. Online proctoring for asynchronous test taking, while not without its problems, has proven effective in preventing cheating at rates comparable to in-person classes (Dendir & Maxwell, 2020). Human oversight is necessary for subjects like English or philosophy, where an essay is required, to provide proper actionable feedback. With the release of ChatGPT and similar large language learning model tools in late 2022, rudimentary actionable feedback on student essays is already available and will only become more useful in the future.

As learning systems become more advanced, we will gain increased knowledge of the many ways in which a student might misunderstand the material and in theory, provide a ready explanation that clicks for them and gets them past any potential speed bumps. Already, we have found that the mixture of student interactions is approximately 1/5th in need of instructional assistance and 4/5th in need of coaching. We divide these modalities by whether a student requires a subject matter expert to be satisfied with their interaction (if so, they need instructional assistance). It is interesting to note that this proportion of instructional assistance and coaching has remained consistent over time. Frequently, the roadblock for students is not content-related but may be related to motivation, confidence, or time management.

When we analyze the 80% of tutoring labeled coaching, we find an enormous opportunity to subdivide this interaction further. The most cost-efficient version of delivering a high-quality experience occurs when a peer-to-peer community can provide the motivation, confidence, and time management help a student needs. An online learning community should be able to serve this function well, just as they do in Fortnite. One possible way to multiply an instructor or coach's capacity is to lead synchronous office hours or a recitation session periodically.

Technology and Pedagogy Curves

A consistent complaint of faculty who teach online courses is the time it takes to come up to speed on new technologies. Particularly for professors newly transitioning from a traditional classroom to an online platform, learning these skills can be overwhelming and can dominate the online teaching experience. For many instructors, though, online technology skills are mastered before the pedagogical skills that are so crucial to a meaningful online learning experience. Faculty who have mastered face-to-face pedagogy are not necessarily able to translate their skills to a different modality (Freeman, 2015).

The time spent *creating* a course depends on the technological, pedagogical, and subject matter knowledge of the instructor, but it also depends on the complexity of the course elements. Content development and pre-semester setup for online courses are more time-consuming than face-to-face courses in general, and online courses are not all created equally. The predominance of a model in higher ed where each instructor creates his or her unique version of each course means that there is a paucity of research about the time required to create different complexities of course elements. We can take a cue from instructional designers, who categorize courses based on the complexity of interactive elements. The time commitment required to produce interactive high-quality content is much greater than the time required to create a basic, non-interactive course (Defelice, 2018).

Table 6.3 Time required in hours to create one hour of content (based on Defelice, 2018)

Type of course	Instructional Designer Hours to Create
Traditional	38
Synchronous virtual	28
Passive (learner as receiver of information)	42
Limited interactivity (simple responses to instructional cues)	71
Complex interactions (multiple and varied responses to cues)	130

More efficient course design

Offloading course creation to a team of instructional designers, then, would have three effects. First, if the instructor is also the course designer, this second role is a significant drain on an instructor's time. If we eliminate that, we can free up an enormous amount of the instructor's time that can be used for other purposes. Second, the course can be more effective pedagogically if it is built by instructional design experts who are well-versed in the pedagogical methods that make online teaching effective, including a space for peer-to-peer interactions. Third, a dedicated team of course designers is more likely to build a high-quality interface that leverages tools in a way that will not detract from student learning. Unskillfully deployed technologies can reduce learning because students, too, need to understand how these technologies are used. It is important to identify specific tools that can be effectively incorporated into a course model. The course should drive the tool selection rather than the other way around, and instructional designers have more tools at their disposal (Scoppio & Luyt, 2017; Tynan, Ryan & Lamont-Mills, 2015).

Conclusions

So where does this all lead? As online technologies for teaching and the art and craft of online instruction improve, more of an instructor's valuable time can be spent teaching students one-on-one, yielding more efficient, superior course experiences for all parties. We are at an inflection point in the industry of education and at the very beginning of our understanding of how existing and future technologies will lead to better outcomes. It is imperative that we embrace these tools and methodologies while carefully assessing their effectiveness to continue the flywheel of innovation in education.

References

Andersen, K. M., & Avery, M. D. (2008). Faculty teaching time: A comparison of web-based and face-to-face graduate nursing courses. *International Journal of Nursing Education Scholarship, 5(1)*. https://doi.org/10.2202/1548-923X.1539

ARM. (2019, November 20). Most popular video games among gamers in the United States in 2019. In *Statista.* Retrieved January 22, 2023, from https://www.treasuredata.com

Bloom, B. (1984). The 2 Sigma Problem: The search for methods of group instruction as effective as one-to-one tutoring. *Educational Researcher,* 13(6), 4–16. https://doi.org/10.2307/1175554

Cavanaugh, J. (2005). Teaching online - A time comparison. *Online Journal of Distance Learning Administration, 8(1)*.

Cifuentes, L., & Hughey, J. (2003). The interactive effects of computer conferencing and multiple intelligences on expository writing. *Quarterly Review of Distance Education, 4(1),* 15–30.

Defelice, R. A. (2018). *How long to develop one hour of training? Updated for 2017.* Association for Talent Development. https://www.td.org/insights/how-long-does-it-take-to-develop-one-hour-of-training-2017

Freeman, L. A. (2015). Instructor time requirements to develop and teach online courses. *Online Journal of Distance Learning Administration, 18(1).*
https://www.westga.edu/~distance/ojdla/spring181/freeman181.html

Lieberman, M. (2019, March 27). Discussion Boards: Valuable? Overused? Discuss. *Inside Higher Ed.*
https://www.insidehighered.com/digital-

learning/article/2019/03/27/new-approaches-discussion-boards-aim-dynamic-online-learning

Marlatt, R. (2020). Capitalizing on the craze of Fortnite: Toward a conceptual framework for understanding how gamers construct communities of practice. *Journal of Education, 200(1),* 3–11. https://doi.org/10.1177/0022057419864531

Martin, F., Kumar, S., Ritzhaupt, A. D., & Polly, D. (2023). Bichronous online learning: Award-winning online instructor practices of blending asynchronous and synchronous online modalities. *The Internet and Higher Education, 56,* 100879. https://doi.org/10.1016/j.iheduc.2022.100879

Ruggles, C., Wadley, G., & Gibbs, M. (2005). Online community building techniques used by video game developers. https://doi.org/10.1007/11558651_12

Scoppio, G., & Luyt, I. (2017). Mind the gap: Enabling online faculty and instructional designers in mapping new models for quality online courses. *Education and Information Technologies, 22(3),* 725–46. https://doi.org/10.1007/s10639-015-9452-y

Twitchtracker. (2022, December 8). Most popular games on Twitch worldwide as of December 2022, by peak all-time viewers (in millions). In *Statista.* Retrieved January 22, 2023, from https://www.twitchtracker.com

Tynan, B., Ryan, Y., & Lamont-Mills, A. (2015). Examining workload models in online and blended teaching. *British Journal of Educational Technology, 46(1),* 5–15.

Uhl-Bien, M., Riggio, R. E., Lowe, K. B., & Carsten, M. K. (2014). Followership theory: A review and research agenda. *The Leadership Quarterly, 25(1),* 83–104. https://doi.org/10.1016/j.leaqua.2013.11

Chapter 7

Elizabeth P. Callaghan

Effective Learning Objectives in the Hybrid Classroom

Abstract

When used in traditional hybrid courses, learning objectives often structure a course's overall shape. However, at the individual class level, connections to learning objectives can be haphazard and indirect at best. This chapter discusses the benefits of using granular learning objectives for each class session in hybrid courses, allowing them to guide learning and connect asynchronous activities with those in a synchronous classroom.

Over the last twenty years, a paradigm shift in higher education has realigned university priorities from teaching to learning models (Fink, 2013; Whetten, 2007). As a result, learning objectives have become common and expected in in-person and online courses. Learning objectives are variously defined, but most educators agree that they are meant to clearly express what skills and knowledge a student should acquire after learning. WASC, the Western Association of Schools and Colleges, now includes learning objectives in their accreditation criteria, describing them as "a concise statement of what the student should know or be able to do" (Schoepp, 2016, p. 616). Indeed, research indicates that learning objectives are effective for both instructional design and student success (Barnard et al., 2021; Stanny, 2016; Whetten, 2007).

With the onset of the pandemic, teaching in higher education was thrown into disarray, and schools were forced to move quickly to online modalities, either live or asynchronous. As the pandemic progressed, there were uneven returns to in-person learning; as outbreaks occurred, many schools moved back and forth from virtual to in-person and developed hybrid approaches. The result has been a haphazard collection of new learning modalities, coupled with the realization of the strengths and weaknesses of in-person and virtual learning. Consequently, the importance of hybrid learning has grown as schools discover the necessity and value of combining the best available learning modalities. However, to leverage the benefits of each learning environment and combine them effectively, instructors must closely connect the learning in each modality; one of the most effective ways to achieve this cohesion is to use learning objectives thoughtfully and judiciously.

However, despite the widespread recognition of the importance of learning objectives, there is surprisingly little agreement among scholars about what to call them. Most often, the terms "outcome," "objective," or "goal" are used interchangeably. For example, Biggs and Tang (2011) and Adelman (2015) use "outcomes," Suskie (2018) and Fink (2013) use "goals," and Spindler (2015) and Whetten (2007) use "objectives." Some scholars try to mitigate confusion by acknowledging the discrepancies in vocabulary; the Carnegie Mellon Eberly Center titles its white paper "The Educational Value of Course-level *Learning Objectives/Outcomes*" (Eberly n.d., emphasis mine), and Barnard et al. (2021) introduce their work as a study of "learning objectives, sometimes known as learning outcomes" (p. 673). I have chosen not to use "learning outcome" because, as Suskie (2018) points out, "While the term learning outcome has become prevalent in American higher education, it can be confusing because it can be used to describe two very different things: an intended or expected learning outcome... and an actual learning outcome or result" (p. 41). Neither do I use "goals," which has traditionally been used for larger, programmatic ambitions, and therefore doesn't have the specificity and granularity of the term "objective"; as Schoepp (2016) points out, "Goals are conceptualized as broader constructs than learning outcomes, more often associated with programs" (p. 617).

Schoepp (2016) also notes that opposition to the term "objective" originated with the move from teacher- to learner-centered education as well as a backlash to "behaviorist underpinnings" that educators saw in the term "objectives."

However, the results of this backlash have waned in recent years, and I find that the term "objective" clearly indicates the skill or knowledge that is intended to be learned rather than already learned. Moreover, the term "objective" no longer seems to indicate an instructor focus (i.e., that the objectives belong to the teacher and not the student). Therefore, I employ "learning objective" (LO) throughout to refer to "a statement describing what and how a student is expected to learn after exposure to teaching" (Biggs and Tang, 2011, p. 113). While some scholars discuss institutional, program, or degree-level learning objectives, I will be referring only to course- and class-session learning objectives. It's at the course and class-session level that learning objectives can connect synchronous and asynchronous learning and activities.

Learning Objective Verbs

Emphasis on learning objectives has led to a large body of scholarship on their effectiveness as well as how to deploy them successfully. Most scholars now agree that learning objectives can improve student learning when used properly and that an effective learning objective includes a specific and measurable verb, content, and context, as Biggs and Tang (2011) layout:

[Learning objectives] need to be stated in such a way that they stipulate:
- the verb at the appropriate level of understanding or of performance intended;
- the topic content the verb is meant to address, the object of the verb in other words;
- the context of the content discipline in which the verb is to be deployed. (pp. 124-125)

The most important part of the LO statement is the verb, which indicates both the mental processing the student should perform and the depth of this mental processing. Greater mental processing requires going through more mental steps, including those required to access information stored in long-term memory and to reason about connections among different facts and concepts. For example, the LO "Define photosynthesis" requires a relatively simple and surface-level form of processing; students need only to learn what photosynthesis is, not how it works or how it interacts with other biological processes. However, "Describe the process of photosynthesis" requires deeper and more complex processing, as the student must understand how photosynthesis actually works. The verb indicates what kind and level of thinking the student should engage in. As Adelman (2015) asserts, "the verb is the center, fulcrum, engine of a learning outcome statement" (p. 7).

The above example is simple, but once we get deeper into learning objective design, choices become less clear and more complex. Consensus exists that verbs must be specific, measurable, and actionable, but there is little agreement on how to achieve this goal, and often, educators don't take the time to choose verbs carefully. As a result, verb choice most often derails a learning objective. Evidence from multiple studies (Barnard et al., 2021; Guilbert, 2002; Schoepp, 2019) indicates that learning objectives are infrequently used to best effect, largely because of the choice of verb.

The greatest challenge in deploying effective learning objectives continues to be how to choose verbs that are specific enough to direct learning reliably but not so granular that they become unwieldy and confusing (or so specific that the resulting knowledge is unlikely to transfer even to closely related situations). Schoepp's (2019) study found that the "quality of learning outcomes is quite poor," largely because instructors are "using non-measurable verbs, lacking or having too much specificity, or having a combination of a non-measurable verb and lacking or having too much specificity" (p. 615, p. 621).

Many institutions still rely on Bloom's taxonomy to categorize learning objective verbs, hoping that Bloom's hierarchy will help instructors guide students to perform "higher-level thinking." However, verbs frequently associated with Bloom's categories are often non-measurable and vague (e.g., "understand"), undermining the effectiveness of the learning objective. Moreover, the framework often fails to reliably indicate a level of cognitive difficulty because there is "considerable variability in how specific verbs align with categories" (Stanny, 2016). In fact, in Stanny's (2016) study of lists of measurable verbs aligned with Bloom's categories, she found that "No verb was assigned consistently to the same category by all 30 lists in the sample. Many lists in the sample duplicated verbs and listed them in two or more categories" (p. 4). Moreover, Stanny notes that there are often "multiple interpretations of the level of skill described by a verb" (p. 7), therefore leaving the choice of level of thinking up to the student (who, incidentally, usually chooses the path of least resistance).

Other scholars have found similar difficulties with both Bloom's taxonomy and Bloom's revised taxonomy (Doughty, 2006; Stanny, 2016), and several have proposed their own taxonomies, such as Fink's (2013) Taxonomy of Significant Learning or Marzano and Kendall's (2008) Taxonomy of Educational Objectives. Taxonomies seek to categorize learning objective verbs into levels of cognitive difficulty, but ultimately, this categorization doesn't significantly improve learning objectives. Focusing too much on classifying verbs misses the fundamental problem: choosing verbs that are specific and measurable so that students understand what they need to do with information, and instructors can design assessments that evaluate whether students have indeed achieved the learning objective. Having specificity is even more important in the hybrid classroom, where access to instructors and further clarification isn't always available.

In order, then, to ensure that a learning objective has a specific and measurable verb, instructors should ask themselves how they would measure whether or not a student has achieved the objective; that is, whether a student has, in fact, learned what the instructor wanted them to learn. As Adelman (2105) recommends, "For every verb-driven learning outcome statement you write, offer three different examples of assignments that flow logically from the governing verbs of the statement" (p. 8). For example, if a learning objective asks students to "Understand the political system of the Roman Empire," we should ask: how will the instructor know that a student understands? This question might lead us to clarify that students should "Describe the political system of the Roman Empire," which is more specific and measurable (students could, for example, write a description of the centralized imperial authority and its powers in relation to the Senate, etc.). Pursuing this refinement, instructors might further specify that they want students to "Compare the roles of the Emperor and the Senate during the Roman Empire," which specifies even further the kind of mental processing students will be expected to perform on the content.

In the hybrid classroom, specific and measurable verbs direct students about how to approach their asynchronous work to prepare them for the synchronous classroom. Using the above example, with the learning objective "Describe the political system of the Roman Empire," students doing asynchronous reading or video viewing know to focus primarily on content about the political system. They may read or watch content that also discusses religious life, the social order, or art, but with a learning objective to guide them, students can direct their learning to foreground specific content. With the even more specific learning objective in the last example, students would understand that they should be able to describe the Roman Senate and Emperor during the Roman Empire and be able to compare their powers, roles, and responsibilities. Having this focus while working through asynchronous material prepares students for their synchronous activities and maximizes learning and practice during that time.

Session-Level Learning Objectives

The success of this approach is contingent upon students understanding the connection between the learning objective and their work, both asynchronous and synchronous, which is why granular, class-level learning objectives are desirable in a hybrid classroom. In an in-person-only classroom, there is always room for an instructor to clarify objectives or field student questions. The hybrid classroom, which uses asynchronous activities that don't necessarily allow for immediate clarification from an instructor, can be just as unambiguous by employing class session-level learning objectives.

Current research indicates that LOs are used both for course design and student direction, but most frequently, LOs are deployed at a degree, program, or course level. However, using class session-level LOs can improve both course design and student learning. As an instructor designs a course, breaking course-level LOs into class-session objectives ensures that the entirety of a larger objective is covered; in addition, it directs the instructor to decompose a larger concept or skill into its component parts, thereby guiding students more systematically toward achievement and ensuring that there are no missed skills or knowledge. As an example, Table 1 shows how a larger course-level LO is broken down into class-session objectives. By decomposing the course-level LO into smaller, more granular LOs for each class session, instructors help ensure that all aspects of a topic are covered. Moreover, granular LOs provide a map for students to understand how to achieve the larger objective. Here, students understand that in order to analyze the relationship between supply, demand, and market equilibrium, they must achieve all of the granular LOs.

Table 7.1 Course-level learning objectives and corresponding class-level objectives

Course-level LO: Analyze the relationship between supply, demand, and market equilibrium.	
Class 1 LO:	Explain the law of demand, the law of supply, and equilibrium.
Class 2 LO:	Identify and analyze a demand curve and a supply curve.
Class 3 LO:	Describe factors that affect supply and demand.
Class 4 LO:	Create a demand curve and illustrate changes in demand.
Class 5 LO:	Create a supply curve and illustrate changes in supply.

Class-level LOs in a hybrid classroom also connect the asynchronous work with its synchronous counterpart. By providing an LO for a specific class session, instructors direct students to focus on specific aspects of the assigned content. For example, in a history class, students might read a chapter on Imperial Rome before the class session. Without a specific LO, students will likely give everything in the chapter equal weight, or they may haphazardly focus on sections they find most important or interesting. Now, let's imagine this assignment attached to the class-level LO, "Compare economic and political factors leading to the decline of the Roman Empire." In this case, students understand that they should pay closer attention to these factors and less attention to others, such as the rise and legalization of Christianity (a religious factor) or the decline of the army (a military factor). With this focus, students are well-prepared to participate in activities in the synchronous classroom that help achieve this LO.

Finally, using class-level LOs helps to mitigate the challenges of choosing the perfect verb for a given objective. Because each course-level objective has several corresponding class-session objectives, the meaning of the course-level verb can be defined more precisely. The verb "analyze" subsumes many mental processes, such as comparing and contrasting, differentiating, or evaluating. To do each of these, students must first be able to identify, define, or explain related concepts. Therefore, by using smaller, more targeted LOs, decomposed from larger course-level objectives, instructors can refine the skills and knowledge they want students to acquire. In addition, these class-level objectives provide students with a straightforward map for attaining knowledge and skills. In the hybrid classroom, this thorough direction helps ensure that students target their work efficiently and are prepared for all learning activities.

Case Study: Developing Course and Class-Session LOs

To illustrate the development of granular session-level LOs, we can take a sample hybrid course and follow the steps to create robust, effective, and productive LOs to guide student learning. In this case study, we will briefly develop the learning objectives for a course on 20th-century American literature. To begin, we must create course-level learning objectives, which can be achieved in a number of ways. Some schools might have departmental course-level objectives; some instructors may choose to brainstorm a list of things they want students to know by the end of the course. One helpful strategy is to ask, "How do I want students to be different at the end of this course?" In this example, I might decide I want students to know what modernism and postmodernism are, be able to analyze and interpret 20th-century literature and connect literary works to their historical, social, and cultural contexts. This gives us three areas with which to create course-level learning objectives. In this initial stage, don't limit yourself to writing targeted learning objectives; your goal is to decide what you want students to learn, and once you've determined that, you can focus on translating those ideas into meaningful learning objectives.

Once we've brainstormed, we can translate these ideas into effective course-level learning objectives. In doing so, we should be certain to employ all the best practices for LOs, with the knowledge that they should be broad enough to encompass all we want students to learn but specific enough to be measurable and clear. The following chart shows the movement from our initial brainstorm to effective course-level LOs:

Table 7.2 Brainstorm to course-level LOs

How students should be different (brainstorm)	Course-level LOs
know what modernism and postmodernism are connect literary works to their historical, social, and cultural contexts be able to analyze and interpret 20th-century literature	Identify and analyze historical, social, and cultural influences on American modernism.
	Characterize modernism and modernist texts in 20th-century American literature.
	Interpret modernist American literature using textual analysis.
	Identify and analyze historical, social, and cultural influences on American postmodernism.
	Characterize postmodernism and postmodern texts in 20th-century American literature.
	Interpret postmodern American literature using textual analysis.

Here, we've taken our initial thoughts about what students should learn and turned them into course-level objectives that will provide a skeleton for the rest of the course. This step can take many forms; in this instance, we've divided the course into modernism (the first three course-level LOs) and postmodernism (the second three course-level LOs), but we could have chosen a different organization, such as a thematic approach (for example, creating course-level objectives about war poetry, the Harlem Renaissance, surrealism, etc.). As with any writing process, it's important to remember that once you've created these course-level objectives, they aren't written in stone; rather, as you decompose them into smaller, session-level LOs, you may discover that you need to revise them, add to them, or even eliminate some.

Once we have a draft of course-level objectives, we can begin to break them down into session-level LOs. We do this by asking: "What exactly must a student know or be able to do to achieve this course-level objective thoroughly?" So, let's begin with our first course-level LO: "Identify and analyze historical, social, and cultural influences on American modernism." We can decompose this LO into smaller, session-length LOs (noting that some sessions might have more than one LO, some session-length LOs might require more than one session, and there will be variance in the number of session-level LOs required to achieve a course-level LO):

Table 7.3 Course-Level LO broken down to Session-level LOs

Course-Level LO	Session-Level LOs
Identify and analyze historical, social, and cultural influences on American modernism.	Characterize the effect of WWI on American modernist literature.
	Characterize the effect of the Great Depression on American modernist literature.
	Describe and analyze the ways urbanization and industrialization affected American modernist literature.
	Describe and analyze the ways existentialism affected American modernist literature.
	Analyze the ways in which American modernist writers challenged traditional hierarchies of race, class, sex, and wealth.
	Characterize the ways in which jazz and modernist visual art affected American modernist literature.

We would then repeat the process with all the other course-level LOs, iterating and revising until we have a complete picture of the LOs that students will grapple with in each class session.

Once each class session has an LO, both instructors and students can use them as a guide. For instructors, all activities, assignments, and assessments should align tightly with the session-level LOs. For example, when characterizing the effect of WWI on American modernist literature, the instructor might create an activity where students compare first-hand accounts of trench warfare with imagery in a selection from T. S. Eliot's *The Waste Land*; when characterizing the effect of the Great Depression on American modernist literature, students might debate whether racial oppression or economic instability were more influential on Langston Hughes' "Let America Be America Again." In addition, guiding LOs for each session assist the instructor in focusing all the resources for that session. In a hybrid course, when some material is housed online, some delivered in person, some synchronous, and others asynchronous, a guiding LO works to coordinate resources consistently. For students, knowing specific LOs for each class session can help them prepare their asynchronous work: reading, assignments, or other content sources (videos, podcasts, etc.). Knowing, for instance, that a class session would be focusing on urbanization and industrialization leads students to pay close attention to these aspects of whatever texts they may be addressing.

Conclusion

The use of granular learning objectives in hybrid courses has the potential to transform how students approach and engage with course materials. By breaking down course-level LOs into smaller, more manageable sets of session-level LOs, teachers can ensure that each class session is connected to the larger goals of the course in a meaningful and effective way. This specificity not only improves student learning and engagement but also helps to bridge the gap between asynchronous and synchronous learning activities, creating a more cohesive and effective learning experience. By implementing granular learning objectives, teachers can create a more focused and purposeful hybrid course, maximizing the benefits of both synchronous and asynchronous learning environments.

References

Adelman, C. (2015). *To imagine a verb: The language and syntax of learning outcomes statements.* Occasional Paper No. 24; University of Illinois and Indiana University, National Institute for Learning Outcomes Assessment.

Allan, J. (1996). Learning outcomes in higher education. *Studies in Higher Education 21*(1), 93–108.

Biggs, J., and C. Tang. (2011). *Teaching for quality learning at university* (4th ed.). Maidenhead: Open University Press.

Barnard, M., Whitt, E. & McDonald, S. (2021). Learning objectives and their effects on learning and assessment preparation: insights from an undergraduate psychology course. *Assessment & Evaluation in Higher Education 46*(5), 673-684.

Doughty, H. A. (2006). Blooming idiots: Educational objectives, learning taxonomies and the pedagogy of Benjamin Bloom. *College Quarterly 9*(4), n.p.

Fink, L. D. (2013). *Creating significant learning experiences: An integrated approach to designing college courses.* John Wiley & Sons, Incorporated.

Guilbert, J.-J. (2002). The ambiguous and bewitching power of knowledge, skills, and attitudes leads to confusing statements of learning objectives. *Education for Health: Change in Learning & Practice 15*(3), 362–369.

Schoepp, K. (2019). The state of course learning outcomes at leading universities. *Studies in Higher Education 44*(4), 615-627.

Spindler, M. (2015). Collaborative analysis and revision of learning objectives. *NACTA Journal, 59*(2), 111–115.

Stanny, C.J. (2016). Reevaluating Bloom's taxonomy: What measurable verbs can and cannot say about student learning. *Education Sciences 6*(4), 37.

Whetten, D. A. (2007). Principles of effective course design: What I wish I had known about learning-centered teaching 30 years ago. *Journal of Management Education 31*(3), 339–357.

Chapter 8

Shaunak Roy and Brian Verdine

Hybrid Learning Across Time and Space

Abstract

In the modern educational world, especially coming out of a raging pandemic, the distinctions between in-person and online and between synchronous and asynchronous learning have become increasingly blurred. At the same time, online or asynchronous portions of a learning experience design can easily feel disjointed from the synchronous or in-person elements, making it difficult to truly blend learning for students working at different times and in different places. Discussion board assignments or the use of other interactive technology tools are a common attempt to bridge this gap, but often these tools are not incorporated meaningfully into courses and are underused, or the assignments feel like busywork. In either case, they do little to increase positive student interactions with peers and instructors. At worst, they lead to more disengagement rather than being a solution to it. This chapter explores various high-impact pedagogical practices, technology and design choices, and game design principles that build strong learning communities. These communities, and the authentic connections they facilitate, are key to successful learning across hybrid modalities because they keep students and instructors motivated and interested, improve course progression, and increase "contact time" with the material. That increased engagement, along with the cooperation that emerges as authentic connections form in communities, is especially vital for effective interaction. Regardless of whether they are online or in-person, effective interactive course elements require students to be thoughtful and active co-creators of a quality learning experience for each other.

Hybrid Learning Across Time and Space

Did you know that for successful business executives, it has been estimated that only 10% of their learning has happened through formal instruction? That finding is based on a survey researching the key developmental experiences of successful managers (Lombardo & Eichinger, 1996). They concluded that the bulk of learning happens outside of formal classes, with 20% happening through social interactions and 70% happening from experiential learning opportunities where new knowledge is created and used in real-world applications. Those proportions do not hold in all situations for all groups of people, and the model has been criticized for how broadly the so-called "70-20-10 rule" has been applied despite how narrow the sample of collected data. Nonetheless, the implication, which is supported by additional extensive educational literature, is that "practicing" or applying knowledge in context (Billett, 2010) and having the opportunity to learn with others (Okita et al., 2007) will tend to promote more or deeper learning. How can we incorporate these social and experiential learning opportunities into courses? How can we build in human interaction, especially when students are increasingly demanding online, asynchronous, or hybrid learning approaches? We believe that the answer, which we will be exploring throughout this chapter, is to build and immerse students in strong, multi-purpose, continuously-active learning communities.

What Do Learning Communities Offer for Active Learning?

The very distinctions between in-person and online, and synchronous and asynchronous learning, are dissolving to the point where *most* courses are in some way "hybrid." Emerging from the pandemic and staring down the 2025 "enrollment cliff" (Kline, 2019), many on-ground programs are being forced by students and economic realities to evaluate their current teaching and learning practices. This is leading to rapid changes and innovative strategies emerging in an industry that relies heavily on tradition and, due to its own success, has not historically needed to evolve to increase its enrollments. While some of this change is very obviously bad, and change is often scary, the upside is that this particular moment in time represents a historic opportunity to not only imagine what could be possible in education but breathe life into that vision. It is an opportunity to improve upon past teaching methods and replace anything that we recognize is sub-optimal or yielding questionable results.

As we do this, many programs are grappling with students who are now used to having options to attend online and are requesting hybrid options despite campuses re-opening (Lempres, 2022; McKenzie, 2021). In-person or synchronous learning certainly maintains a level of popularity among instructors, students, and parents. Likely, they assume it will lead to a better learning experience that meets more basic psychological needs, an assumption with supporting evidence (Fabriz et al., 2021). Sharing physical spaces would seem more likely to promote authentic human connections and enable students to have the positive aspects of the "traditional college experience" portrayed in popular culture. When we talk about authentic human connections throughout this chapter, we are referring to the kinds of experiences in which students can interact regularly and "socially" enough with others to build actual friendships while working together learning a topic. The kind of friendships with peers and instructors that cement into lifelong social and professional networks. One fear among some educators aside from any specific experience students might miss by not being on campus, is that learners who are not in close physical proximity to others can easily become hopelessly "lost" on their educational pathway. On campus or attending synchronous sessions, students can supposedly get help and motivation in real-time from the instructor or other students. The COVID-19 pandemic certainly put a spotlight on the various ways that human connections are important for our mental health and happiness (Okabe-Miyamoto & Lyubomirsky, 2021), not to mention our learning (Boud et al., 2013). Yet more students than ever want hybrid learning options (Barnes & Noble College, 2022; Samson, 2022). Why would students now want to opt-out of showing up to class and connecting with peers and their instructor, if they have the option to attend class?

Our guess at the answer is a simple deduction. Since students appear to value connecting with their peers and instructors but are insisting on having options to avoid class, maybe it is because they are not interacting very much or making authentic connections in most classes. Maybe most students do not actually feel like their class offers opportunities to connect with their instructor and peers or to feel like an important part of the class. Many probably do not want to walk across campus because being there offers little more opportunity to connect with others than a recorded lecture. Or maybe they feel they have as good a chance of their instructor answering an email question as they do of getting a chance to ask their question during class.

Perhaps the reality is that most authentic connections tend to grow out of the less teaching-focused and more social settings of a campus. A student lounge. The quad. The dining commons. Or even clubs, interest groups, or research labs, where students are surrounded by peers with similar goals and shared interests who are less likely to judge them. All of these are spaces where people are better able to interact and express themselves as individuals. Regardless, we can probably safely conclude that if attending most classes really was meeting social needs, building soft skills that impacted their success, and providing social and experiential learning experiences, then it is doubtful students would be asking to skip them (Samson, 2022).

Many heroic instructors do take it upon themselves to create an incredibly social and experiential learning environment in their on-ground classrooms. Nonetheless, even in these seemingly ideal synchronous spaces and with a committed and experienced instructor, class sizes beyond 10 or 20 students make most interactive activities difficult. Many courses also have only 2 or 3 synchronous sessions weekly for a few hours in total. If a class lasts 60 minutes, simply trying to organize and instruct 20 students to do an activity could waste 10 of them. Trying to organize 300 students... well, we do not like to say anything is impossible! The reality, though, is that creating opportunities for peers to connect while handling the "business" of a class is challenging. Even if an instructor is well-intended and highly interactive, class time is usually fixed. Simple mathematics tells us that as the number of students goes up but class time stays constant, each student will get a little less personal attention from the instructor and less time to connect with peers; unless the instructor can extend these opportunities outside class.

Even under ideal circumstances, most instructors know the blank stares and silence they get when starting a class conversation, especially from students who are unfamiliar with each other. Not to mention shy, under-confident, or non-native speaking students, who often find it intimidating to participate. Class conversations may not be as inclusive as we hope, even when the conditions appear optimal; alternative ways to participate often allow certain students to find a voice that would be silent in a synchronous classroom (Lempres, 2022).

Fostering authentic interaction and building a learning community among students is challenging because it requires things like willing participation from learners, time, openness, vulnerability, a shared mission, and true cooperation. Still, cultivating a true sense of community among students is important for motivation and does appear to buffer them from things like poor academic outcomes and depression, which can be particularly important for underrepresented minority and first-generation students who tend to report a lower sense of belonging at their institutions (e.g., Gopalan et al., 2022). Online or hybrid courses that do not address these student needs risk negative impacts on learning, and these courses will tend to create more dropout among those already at higher risk of poor educational outcomes. Even if students are "well-connected" on their campus and have a strong sense of belonging at their institution, communities will usually have positive impacts on courses; almost everything becomes easier when students feel motivated and are willing to help one another. This may be especially true in the hybrid modality where students' virtual engagement with each other and the instructor can feed more productive live sessions and vice versa.

Tawnya Means, Ph.D., now Assistant Dean for Educational Innovation and Chief Learning Officer at the University of Illinois Urbana-Champaign, told us in a recent e-book interview that, "The impact of COVID has touched every single institution of learning, globally — from preschool to higher education, not to mention its impact on countless other organizations. The experience of shifting all education to remote and hybrid delivery has taught us that the right technology is not a 'nice to have' but a necessity. High quality, evidence-based pedagogical tools for delivering learning experiences, maintaining engagement, supporting interaction, and building and maintaining community are vital to creating disruption-proof education" (Yellowdig, 2021a, p. 12). This is a sentiment we are certain is shared among many educators and institutions as we leave the pandemic behind. But can technology really help us form a learning community and *authentic* connections among our learners?

Technology Is Part of the Solution

Technology can help build authentic connections across hybrid learning environments, but it requires a shift in thinking, intentional design, and evidence-based iteration. Most importantly, these things must happen for both the design of educational technology and our learning experiences. We will further argue that building authentic connections becomes much easier by implementing proven practices in game design for both technologies and courses. Most of the base principles of Yellowdig, our patented point system, and our recommendations for community management draw inspiration from games. While many other technologies and educational experiences incorporate gameful learning principles (e.g., GradeCraft, developed by the University of Michigan), it remains a field that is far too often ignored in education. For example, a core tenet of gameful learning is providing students with increased self-determination because of its ability to foster motivation (Deci & Ryan, 2000; Ryan & Deci, 2020).

As the Founder and a VP of Yellowdig, we have each seen success in building learning communities for tens of thousands of courses and programs with these gameful approaches. We will be using some examples from the Yellowdig experience as case studies here, but the lessons extend well beyond what we have done. When we combine intentional, iterative, and game-based design with thoughtful instructors and awareness of the needs and motivations of students, technology becomes a powerful driver of student connection and learning. A reason that students want hybrid courses using technology (e.g., Jenay, 2021) is that educational technology has matured to the point that it offers obvious conveniences and advantages for learning that cannot be matched by a brick-and-mortar classroom alone (e.g., increased options for contact time with the material and instructor). Thoughtfully designed hybrid courses end up offering more choices for students (we talk about the importance of this gameful design concept later) and more ways for them to interact more often with the content, peers, and their instructor.

Are Discussion Board Interactions Creating Community?

Before we go deeper into gameful learning and lessons we learned at Yellowdig, let us explore one of the currently established approaches to building interaction in hybrid courses. Discussion boards are a common attempt to bridge the gap between synchronous and asynchronous learning to create more space for social and experiential learning. But how often do you hear anyone actually excited about them? Our answer is very rarely. Students tend to mock them (Martinez, 2019). Instructors and course designers spill endless ink on how to create better prompts and avoid difficulties in managing them (e.g., Gernsbacher, 2016; Lieberman, 2019), often with eye-catching titles that acknowledge a shared negative sentiment like "The Ever Dreaded Discussion Board – Out of the Box Activities and How to Handle the Workload" (Grady, 2020) or "Why Online Discussion Boards Suck, and What to Do About It" (Lane, 2020).

The prototypical discussion board approach features instructors mandating a posted response to a prompt and students commenting on two other posts by midnight on Sunday. How commonly do students finish their discussion assignment at the last minute, right before it is due? Most instructors seem to know this is a concern, but maybe not how serious it is. In the early days of Yellowdig's Classic platform, we naively enabled a discussion-style framework and had not yet implemented many of our current gameful strategies to spread out student participation. Web traffic regularly spiked 50-100x normal on Sunday evening as students flooded into our platform dutifully responding to their discussion assignments. Ignoring many other concerns, a huge problem is that unlike non-interactive assignments (e.g., papers, science labs, problem sets, etc.), if enough students procrastinate and do all of the work at one time, it becomes *literally impossible* to achieve an asynchronous back-and-forth discussion; every student that participates that way is posting and reacting to other students' posts as required, but not truly interacting with anyone. Because they are not, they are unquestionably not making authentic human connections while simultaneously reducing the value of the exercise for everyone else.

Acknowledging this problem, a very common approach for improving discussions, which does seem to at least help ensure peers have something to react to, is adding a deadline earlier in the week for creating an initial response to the prompt. These second deadlines do ensure that posts are completed early enough in the week that students can read them, allowing the possibility of discussing them (e.g., Gernsbacher, 2016). As downsides, they also give students another thing to worry about on a weekly basis and give instructors another rule to enforce. Finding it a little odd to try to solve a problem created by deadlines by implementing more deadlines, we dealt with these problems with gameful solutions: we incentivized early participation and revisiting to continue conversations, created a "point buffer" that effectively removed hard deadlines, made comments worth more per word than posts in our default point rules, structured our feed to give students more choice, and allowed conversations to end naturally, rather than stop at the end of each week.

In the interactions we have, the majority of instructors complain that their students do not care about discussion assignments or are doing the least they can to get their grades. While that may sound like a typical complaint about students, what it tells us is that simply using interactive technology is not magically motivational or valued educationally by learners. Our earlier reference to student Tweets about discussion boards (Martinez, 2019) readily illustrates why; the Tweets mock the long, text-heavy, repetitive posts that discussion boards generate. These spaces are often filled with unnecessary words to meet a word count and vapid comments filled with platitudes, a common result of students treating the task as busywork.

Unfortunately, in this model, instructors then need to spend their precious time wading through and grading the uninspired posts and "I agree" comments. Ultimately, we find many instructors start to regard discussions as their own form of busywork, resenting time that could be better used on other teaching projects, their research, or departmental service. Interestingly, with their role in discussion boards defined as the question asker and answer grader, in our experience, those who do use this model will usually not consider that they could or should join the discussion and interact with students. We note that anecdotal observation here because there is an important side effect of grading discussions; grading but not taking part in discussions place the instructor into a clear antagonist role (i.e., makes them "Darth Grader"). This seems particularly problematic because these online spaces are one of the few parts of a course where an instructor would otherwise have guaranteed opportunities to interact with and appear helpful to their students. Students also tend to act as if they have to be careful about everything they say when they are being graded, likely because if they show uncertainty or lack of knowledge, they risk it hurting their grades.

As importantly, the grading rarely seems to compel better or more thoughtful conversation while also being of questionable utility as a summative assessment. We talk later about why the typical discussion board grading does not lead to better discussions, but it is important to discuss why it is not a valid individual student assessment. First, the assessment is not usually measuring the learner's ability to take part in a good discussion. It focuses on their ability to answer an instructor's prompt, which means it is not a valid assessment of discussion skills. On top of that problem, the task is social, and students are able to see each other's answers to the prompts before they make them. That means what previous students have said influences how students respond, and they frequently alter what they want to say to say something novel. At base, that means their posts are not an accurate, valid, or "pure" reflection of *their* personal knowledge of the topic either.

Some instructors and technologies hide initial responses until everyone has made them, which negates this problem but creates another one that hurts engagement and discussion; the initial responses to the prompt will tend to be even more repetitive and make the same point repeatedly. That is not a winning recipe for kickstarting a vibrant conversation. One of our Success Managers also once jokingly said: "Assessing discussion quality by grading discussion posts is like rating a book by scoring each page." Discussions are organic, and contributions build on each other. It is difficult to grade that, but if we do, we need to be giving students points for the things we really want to see, like authentic student interactions, "real" conversations, or actions that build a stronger sense of course community.

Many discussion boards are failing to achieve the goals their designers intended, but this is not the way it has to be. We can get our students intrinsically motivated if we pay attention to their needs and what actually interests them (Ryan & Deci, 2020), then use that motivation to help create learning environments that they enjoy and *want* to take part in. That's not easy. It requires a thoughtful approach that motivates them, respects their agency as humans, enables them to feel competent and capable of mastery, and helps them fulfill their needs and goals, especially in largely asynchronous hybrid designs.

Taking Lessons from Games

Have you seen a kid (or adult, for that matter) who needs encouragement to play their favorite game? Usually, encouragement is needed to get them to take a break! Game designers need to build engaging games to make money and, therefore, base the mechanics and gameplay on deeply rooted human psychology. While many popular games are of questionable educational value in the academic sense, almost all good games rely on players learning or improving to progress or win. Many of the best games actually use learning and achievement to promote continued engagement, which is probably exactly the opposite of how most educators think. Educators usually talk of engagement (i.e., attentive participation) to increase learning. The reality is that these two things create an intertwined feedback loop; game design strategies often promote both engagement and learning. Also, while engagement may not be a primary goal for learning, it is practically a prerequisite for it. Attention is vital for memory formation (Chun & Turk-Browne, 2007), and Posner and Rothbart start their paper, *Attention to Learning of School Subjects*, by saying, "Of all the factors that influence learning, attention to the learned material may be the most important" (Posner & Rothbart, 2014, p 14). If students are not engaged in the intended activities while they are completing parts of a course, they are probably not learning, and if they are not learning, they will probably start to disengage.

Rewards Shape Behavior

Rewards and gamification in learning are as old as grades, so the concept of applying rewards and motivating design principles to courses is certainly not new. Grades are rewards according to either of the definitions offered by Mirriam-Webster: 1) Something that is given in return for good or evil done or received or that is offered or given for some service or attainment; or 2) a stimulus (such as food) that is administered to an organism and serves to reinforce a desired response ("Reward," 2022). Grades also have many direct parallels to the rewards that improve games: 1) They motivate the players (i.e., students) to perform better, learn more, try harder, etc., just like collecting coins in a Super Mario Bros. game or wedges in Trivial Pursuit and 2) they signal to others the current skill level or progress of the individual players (i.e., students), just like experience points in role-playing games or Monopoly properties. Students who study more are rewarded with better grades, and better grades help a student "win" at school by affording them a degree and better opportunities. Whether we like it or not, grades are what motivate many students to change from being disengaged from school (e.g., watching Netflix) to sitting down and studying for a test, reading a chapter, or completing a paper.

Feedback and rewards, both of which grades provide, will typically yield behavior change (see definition #2 for "Reward" above). People will do many things for rewards if you give them the information needed to get them, including keeping a safer driving distance (Mazureck & van Hattem, 2006), exercising more (Smeddinck et al., 2019), or shopping more (Keh & Lee, 2006). However, for rewards to work, they do have to be sufficiently rewarding and focused on creating behavior that helps actually achieve the intended goal. For example, in the discussion board paradigm discussed earlier, the reward for participating is grade points for creating a post that answers the instructor's prompt. Many student posts do this pretty well. But answering instructor questions for points is something they can do on a test or quiz. Those points do not reward students for thoughtfully discussing the concept with others but for answering a prompt; students are not motivated by the reward to start spending more time and mental energy discussing because they are not rewarded for that.

In another example of how the wrong rewards may not achieve the intended outcome, we often see that longer posts with more information and complex vocabulary will better fulfill the instructor's rubric, yielding a better grade. However, longer and "denser" posts almost always lead to less conversation, not more. When we used machine learning to study ideal word count settings in our platform, we found requirements for 40-word posts and 20-word comments maximize reading of and subsequent responding to posted content. Recommended post lengths to improve engagement are even shorter in most standard social media (McLachlan, 2022). Reading a post or comment seems necessary to learn something from it, but reading is also required to build a real back-and-forth conversation. Thus well-intentioned instructor rubrics that compel things like 250 words posts and APA citations are probably not generating better discussion *or* as much learning because students read and think less about the content being shared. These requirements, typically intended to try to ensure better learning, may actually be focusing students away from doing the things that would. They are definitely tending to focus them away from producing organic and interesting conversations, building authentic human connections, or developing healthy, cooperative learning communities.

If these things are your goals, students need to be focused on them and rewarded for doing the things that lead to better interactions, like sharing something interesting with their peers that is related to the course and starting a conversation. They need to be then rewarded for coming back to continue conversations and for providing thoughtful replies that are helpful or interesting. Focusing rewards in this way is not *just* about increasing interaction or engagement. If a course designer has chosen to assign a discussion activity for a justifiable educational reason, if the assignment is not yielding a quality discussion, then it would have to be almost sheer luck if the activity was promoting the intended outcomes. Using rewards to encourage the intended behaviors is central to allowing students to access an activity's unique educational benefits.

These principles should be thought of broadly and applied to all manner of student rewards and grading. A great story of how you can use rewards to promote community comes to mind from Lee Pinkowitz, Ph.D., Associate Professor at Georgetown University. As presented in our "Made for Humans" e-book (Yellowdig, 2021b), Dr. Pinkowitz made his community as active as possible by building on top of the Yellowdig point system and distributing awards to students who engaged positively. The awards, like the Postmaster General Award, Helping Hand Award, and Community Builder Award, were based on Yellowdig engagement data from dashboards in our platform. He used those data to incentivize students to be even more collaborative, a behavior change he valued. "I am a believer in collaborative learning. People who put forth an effort to collaborate should be recognized." The reaction from students was so positive that "By week 6 of the course, I was recording award ceremonies in a tux and even had the Dean deliver one of the awards. The students loved it so much. Some of them even recorded acceptance speeches and posted those." Rewarding behaviors that improved cooperation and human connection allowed Dr. Pinkowitz to build a healthier community and ultimately achieve a positive educational experience that everyone seemed to enjoy. It would be hard to know for sure that his students learned better, and he did not collect data to confirm that, but Dr. Pinkowitz certainly perceived his students were benefitting, broadly speaking, from these experiences. Motivation does play a big role in increasing "contact time" with course material and engaged students do tend to retain more (Chun & Turk-Browne, 2007).

Other common and engaging features of games are that they enable players to "choose their own adventure," build their sense of competence as they tackle challenges, and enable players to connect or interact. Players tend to enjoy these things, which are centered around a well-researched psychology theory called Self-Determination Theory (SDT; Deci & Ryan, 2000). SDT suggests there are three things that help create intrinsic motivation - autonomy, competence, and relatedness. The following sections explore these concepts, how they apply to designing and integrating synchronous and asynchronous learning environments for hybrid instruction, and how communities can help add these elements to course designs.

Autonomy

Learning to survive in the *Planet of the Apes* game and learning about astrophysics in Physics 101 probably have more things in common than you might imagine at first. Games like *Planet of the Apes* frequently give players a lot of autonomy, which refers to the feeling of having control over your actions and their consequences. For example, some games allow you to try as many times as you like to jump across a pit your character will fall into every time. As long as the player has options to get around the pit, the player has the autonomy needed for the pit to be an interesting challenge. But if the game gives the player no means to deal with that challenge, they will feel less autonomy, fail more, and be less likely to continue playing. This is why many games allow you to choose to go do something else if you get "stuck," allowing you to come back later with more skills or helpful items.

Although the importance of autonomy in active learning is generally accepted, it is not always clear how to achieve it in learning experience designs. In building a community, providing autonomy starts with cultivating the feeling that the learners matter as human beings and that their point of view is appreciated and encouraged. Autonomy requires a feeling of having control over actions and consequences, so learners need to be encouraged to think for themselves and become co-creators of their own knowledge. They also need to believe they can improve and contribute valid, even if imperfect, thoughts and opinions. Vibrant, low-stakes, and organic discussions are a great way to build a sense of autonomy (and, therefore motivation) while also yielding other benefits from peer and instructor connections.

There is a growing trend in providing "choices" to students in various activities, which can help, but merely giving options does not automatically provide students more control over outcomes. A discussion prompt may be written to provide students with choices of what to talk about, but by and large, those prompts are still doing far more to constrain choice than provide it. Discussion prompts implicitly (if not explicitly) tell students that discussion boards are a place to answer questions, not ask them. They also specify a small list of topics to be discussed. Imagine if a learner is "stuck" on something they needed to learn from two weeks ago while they perfectly understand the current week's topic. Should they have the autonomy to ask a question about an older topic if that is what they need to discuss most? That would certainly give them better control over how they perform on the upcoming test. Obviously, providing students autonomy is a balance, and there may always be things we need to compel students to do, but the reality is that many course designs provide students very little opportunity to control their own participation and miss easy chances to improve motivation via increased autonomy.

In Yellowdig, we typically encourage instructors to forgo discussion prompts and instead ask students to start conversations, ask questions, and bring interesting and relevant things from their real-world experiences to share. Research with our partners comparing implementations within our own technology has repeatedly shown that this community model tends to produce about 50% more overall participation than a discussion board model. Importantly, students can focus on the things they need to learn or are most interested in, which has positive learning and motivational impacts. In a study performed by Fort Hays State University using Yellowdig (Martin et al., 2017), they analyzed different student actions to try to understand how their students engaged with Yellowdig and what was most associated with learning. Engagement in Yellowdig was correlated with course grade outcomes, which is not surprising, but the type of engagement most associated with course grades was not generating posts but "out-degree" connections (i.e., comments on or reactions to other students' posts). These behaviors were interpreted by the authors to be associated with more reading. This outcome should be less surprising than it is to many; most of us know a "lurker" (i.e., someone that never posts) on social media that still knows everything happening with their friends. As educators, our tendency is to believe we know what is best for students and that requiring a "quality" response to a specific topic must be the best way to direct learning in an online discussion. However, when you empower students with real autonomy, they gain more ability to do the things they need; sometimes, those things that are most beneficial to them are surprising to us.

A great way to jump-start building autonomy in an online community is by asking learners to introduce themselves and explain their motivations behind learning a subject. Another good practice, especially for hybrid courses, is to encourage them to start talking about topics early or to blend topics together. Instructors can then pick a top conversation and use it as a springboard for discussion in a synchronous session. This technique allows instructors to celebrate students who are making good use of their autonomy to contribute thoughtfully to the community, which motivates others to do the same, improving the overall value of the community for everyone. Likewise, it allows instructors to incorporate student-driven topics they know learners care about into courses, building a greater sense among students that they are responsible for their own learning and are co-constructors of their learning experience.

Competence

Competence is the ability to do something successfully or efficiently. Building competence is similar to mastery, which George Leonard (1992) defined as "the mysterious process during which what is at first difficult becomes progressively easier and more pleasurable through practice." That an author talking about building competence would describe the process as "pleasurable" is noteworthy because taking a competence-focused or mastery-focused approach to learning is also incredibly powerful for improving. However, for learners to strive for competence, two things are almost a prerequisite from a design standpoint. First is the ability to "safely" fail. The second is the ability to get frequent feedback. One reason many games are so "addictive" is that they allow their players to fail endlessly but "safely." Video-game-addiction.org (*What Makes a Video Game Addictive?*, 2019) describes this compelling aspect of many games like this: "Games that hook players are often designed to be just difficult enough to be truly challenging while allowing players to achieve small accomplishments that compel them to keep playing. In that respect, the design of video games is similar to the design of gambling casinos, which will allow players to have small "wins" that keep them playing." Though obviously, addiction is a problem and certainly not the goal of most educational experience designs, disengagement and disinterest in an educational experience will also have many, many negative social, financial, and educational ramifications. As educators, the courses we deliver are competing against other activities that use these techniques to capture the attention of students, and whether we like it or not, the efficacy of our learning experience designs is impacted by our ability to keep their attention. Our best chance to compete for that attention is to reference these techniques that work from industries that rely on attention to drive their business.

When your character dies in a video game, they usually respawn just a little bit back from where they left off, with few other long-term impacts. Cycles of safe failure allow the player to get fast and clear feedback on what things worked and didn't. Eventually, the player figures out what they need to do or builds new skills, which the game rewards them for by allowing them to get to the next level or challenge. As players traverse the game, the competence they achieve usually brings a sense of accomplishment and satisfaction (i.e., the "wins" referenced above) and encourages them to continue forward, even in the face of immense challenges. There are practical limits to how much difficulty players will tolerate; if players fail too consistently or the cost of failure is high (e.g., having to start from the beginning with every mistake), players will give up more quickly and be more likely to "rage-quit" (i.e., give up with clear indications of frustration or anger). The internet is replete with lists of games that have not balanced the difficulty very well (e.g., https://www.redbull.com/in-en/10-toughest-games-out-there).

Unfortunately, many learning designs and the way students proceed through them do not promote a competence-focused or "growth mindset" approach to their education. Students are often graded after each waypoint in a course and given a fixed grade. That grade may reflect the student's current skill level, but once awarded, it cannot be improved. That situation means there's no real incentive for the student to go back, learn more, and improve upon past mistakes. In this model for grading, failures are not "safe"; they are permanent. And if students accumulate too many failures, they will have to drop the course and restart from the beginning. Like a game that creates many failures and punishes them severely, that can quickly turn to frustration and quitting. Further, these kinds of situations promote a culture focused on being right or "smart," which can prevent many students from ever even participating at all for fear of being judged if they fail. While you may think this fear would be isolated to low performers, it does apply to high achievers too and even has a recognized name in the academic world: "imposter syndrome" (Sakulku, 2011). Some high-performing students fear that at any moment, they may be found out to be "imposters" that are not smart or accomplished enough to be deserving of where they are.

Fast feedback was also mentioned above as important to building competence, but in many courses, feedback comes days or weeks later.

That may be understandable given instructor workloads, but students are less able to learn from their mistakes and maintain the motivation to master a topic. Slow feedback is contrary to the "frequent and in the moment" learning that tends to promote competence. To top it all off, the culture of micro-grading often seems arbitrary and can easily demotivate someone, especially if a poor grade is permanent, as is usually the case. Most of these things could be altered easily through gameful course design and technology that supports less linear, rule-enforcing, or choice-free course designs.

A very interesting case in point comes from John H. Wilson, a teaching professor at Drexel's Close School of Entrepreneurship. John told us about how he teaches an unconventional course called "Ready, Set, Fail" (Yellowdig, 2021a). Failure is a given for entrepreneurs, and they need to learn to fail and move forward quickly, so John turns things upside down relative to normal grading. Students try entrepreneurial tasks and fail, then talk about what they learned from those failures to get better grades. Much of the collaborative learning comes from students documenting their experiences in Yellowdig and discussing them with peers, exchanging valuable insights on how they transformed their garbage into gold. "That's really what this class is about—teaching them how to fail in a way that will allow them to recover emotionally, financially, and physically." Although it is a unique approach, the philosophy behind it is supported by game design and can be applied, to some extent, in most learning environments.

Participation grading promotes practice and a growth mindset, and it doesn't have to just be about attendance or speaking up during class. Course designers and instructors can award points for participation happening between synchronous sessions as students share interesting posts about course topics, answer other students' questions, etc. Facilitating continuous participation in an asynchronous learning community between synchronous lessons has a number of key advantages. First, all students have ample, regular opportunities to participate. This is simply unachievable in most synchronous classes with more than 10 or 20 students. It also helps certain students who may have more trouble finding their voice in a synchronous setting, like students who are not native speakers or just need a bit more time to compose their thoughts. Second, an asynchronous community enables participation regardless of whether a student can attend or their time zone. Third, online communities can give instructors, course designers, and administrators clear and objective insight into exactly how and how much students are participating. Healthy course communities have a wealth of information needed to help struggling students and make adjustments to teaching during synchronous sessions. All of these things can help instructors be more effective by improving their teaching and extending it beyond limited class time, by helping them see and experience students' "lightbulb moments" that guide teaching, and by improving the likelihood that instructor will be viewed as a helpful "guide-on-the-side" rather than as an antagonistic "grader." Assessment is certainly important, but having some aspects of a course that reward participation and encourage continuous improvement allows students to see that they are on a journey toward competence.

Relatedness

In Self-Determination Theory, relatedness is the need to form strong relationships or bonds with the people around you. According to the theory, such interactions are not only desirable for most people but are essential for their adjustment and well-being. But how often does the average course design focus on helping to create bonds between learners or between learners and the instructor? Is it even the job of an instructor or learning designer who is focused on trying to improve learning to worry about students "bonding" with each other or the instructional team? We would say yes. Though it is not the job of a learning designer or instructor to make students learn, it is their job to focus students on the important things for them to learn and remove as many barricades as possible that would prevent them from learning. Disengagement due to poor student mental health or having a lack of connection to their instructor or peers is a hurdle to learning. That is why, for example, the Department of Education is enforcing new policies for regular and substantive interaction with instructors in online programs (*Regular and Substantive Interaction Refresh*, 2021). But even hybrid and on-ground courses will not automatically fulfill these needs for students just because there may happen to be a synchronous session to attend. "Time and space" for creating authentic interactions will have to be built into courses to ensure these needs are being met.

In our experience, we have seen that providing more "open" community spaces that replace discussion boards tends to lift course completion rates by over 10%, improves course grades for students who do finish, and improves continuation rates to enrollment in the next semester by 5-10% (proprietary partner research conducted between 2019 and 2021, which A-B tested the conversion of over 50 courses with over 5,000 enrolled students). Using our technology to simply replicate discussion board assignments rather than implementing course communities, on the other hand, tends to yield fewer positive impacts. This is because things like modern-looking and intuitive interfaces that work easily are important, but they are not sufficient to change learning outcomes. Adding new technology might automatically make learning more accessible or efficient, but it does not automatically produce more learning if the course design means that students are still doing the same cognitive things they were before the change.

Providing a sense of relatedness is not just about having the potential to form connections; it comes from the actual act of forming and maintaining those meaningful connections with others. Most modern internet-based games achieve this by offering individual gamers the ability to collaborate or compete with one another, usually talking with headsets, chatting, or sharing video feeds. How much are students actually connecting and then maintaining those connections throughout most courses?

Although there are exceptions where courses have been thoughtfully designed to enable connection and maintenance of those connections, many courses are simply not designed with that level of interaction in mind. In most situations, it is simply taken for granted that students will get connected when they need to. That may be true for well-prepared learners and extroverts, but it is not a safe assumption for introverts, first-generation students, those with less college prep, non-native speakers, working students, etc. Incidentally, these types of students are probably those most in need of the motivational and educational benefits of connecting with and learning from others. The challenges some of them face in doing so are also likely a significant source of their higher rates of dropout.

In a blog post by the author of this piece, Dr. Verdine (Verdine, 2020) wrote: "Many degree programs and courses include online discussion board spaces with weekly assignments and prompts to attempt to engage students, promote critical thinking, increase topic relevance, help students network, and allow them to otherwise "interact." Often students and instructors treat these as "check-the-box" assignments, and they rarely spur anything resembling real conversations. Subsequently, these assignments rarely meet their intended educational or social aims." The key takeaway is that even if students are participating in a shared space or on an assignment requiring some student interaction, it does not mean they are really connecting. At least not necessarily in a way that is important for motivation, learning, or student retention.

Leveraging Extrinsic Motivation to Build Intrinsic Motivation

Incorporating the three aspects of Self-Determination Theory (autonomy, competence, and relatedness) that build intrinsic motivation into course design is important for creating an experience that is motivating and fulfills a learner's individual needs. Dr. Pinkowitz, whom we mentioned earlier, was also using extrinsic rewards that helped build relatedness and celebrated people displaying increasing competence. In that way, his extrinsic rewards (points and awards) were helping to encourage an *environment* that provided for the more basic needs of his students, according to SDT. Legitimate concerns about extrinsic rewards include that they can become less effective over time and can interrupt existing intrinsic motivations that people may have for doing something (Deci et al., 1999). However, the example from Dr. Pinkowitz is a good example of how extrinsic rewards like points can be "converted" to intrinsic motivation if done thoughtfully. In instances where we see people building healthy communities with authentic connections between people, students participate much more than is strictly required to get the extrinsic rewards. They are participating extra because they see value in participating, not for a better grade. Incorporating both the SDT elements and the supplemental extrinsic rewards into your attempts to create a course community will typically make those attempts more successful. A community really is needed for an optimal learning experience where members share a common purpose and collective inquiry into a topic of interest, as put forth in the Community of Inquiry framework (a brief description is available at https://coi.athabascau.ca/coi-model/; see also Garrison et al., 1999). To achieve that optimal experience, students must have the ability to project themselves socially, as individuals, into that community. These elements are not just nice to have; they are an integral part of an effective learning experience.

Bridging Gaps Across Time and Space

Classrooms have always existed to form a community that can learn together. In fact, the word "university" itself is derived from the Latin universitas magistrorum et scholarium (Various Authors, 1911). That translates roughly to "community of teachers and scholars." Connecting with others is required for sharing ideas, engaging in healthy debates that expand understanding, and for discussing different points of view. Together this makes community an important enough part of learning that it is effectively indispensable. Community and connection are why even the most advanced scholars form research societies and attend conferences.

And yet our modern educational world has to create optimal learning environments for students who are scattered across space and time. That creates some daunting challenges that we are certainly all familiar with after years of a pandemic. The good news is that we can meet these challenges head-on through a combination of good tools, thoughtful instructional design, high-quality instructors, and respect for the needs and motivations of our learners. We might need only one more thing… to make sure we share the best ideas and learn together!

Author Note

Disclosures: The authors of this piece are both associated with Yellowdig, an educational company focused on building community for education-focused organizations. The conclusions found in this piece are from experiences the authors have had implementing Yellowdig's technology platform and studying community-building strategies with over 150 partner institutions. The authors share specific details, quotes, and citations where possible and have made every attempt to provide clarity and transparency about their data sources, barring extenuating circumstances (e.g., non-disclosure agreements).

Correspondence concerning this article should be addressed to: Shaunak Roy, Yellowdig, 1617 JFK Blvd, 20th Floor, Philadelphia, PA 19103. Email: shaunak@yellowdig.com

References

Barnes & Noble College. (2022). *College 2030™ - Emerging from the Pandemic: Reimagining Higher Education.* https://www.bncollege.com/insight/report/college2030/

Billett, S. (2010). Learning Through Practice. In S. Billett (Ed.), *Learning Through Practice: Models, Traditions, Orientations and Approaches* (pp. 1–20). Springer Netherlands. https://doi.org/10.1007/978-90-481-3939-2_1

Boud, D., Cohen, R., Sampson, J., & (all of the University of Technology, Sydney, Australia) (Eds.). (2013). *Peer Learning in Higher Education: Learning from and with Each Other.* Routledge. https://doi.org/10.4324/9781315042565

Chun, M. M., & Turk-Browne, N. B. (2007). Interactions between attention and memory. *Current Opinion in Neurobiology, 17*(2), 177–184. https://doi.org/10.1016/j.conb.2007.03.005

Deci, E. L., Koestner, R., & Ryan, R. M. (1999). A meta-analytic review of experiments examining the effects of extrinsic rewards on intrinsic motivation. *Psychological Bulletin, 125*, 627–668. https://doi.org/10.1037/0033-2909.125.6.627

Deci, E. L., & Ryan, R. M. (2000). The "what" and "why" of goal pursuits: Human needs and the self-determination of behavior. *Psychological Inquiry, 11*(4), 227–268. https://doi.org/10.1207/S15327965PLI1104_01

Fabriz, S., Mendzheritskaya, J., & Stehle, S. (2021). Impact of synchronous and asynchronous settings of online teaching and learning in higher education on students' learning experience during COVID-19. *Frontiers in Psychology, 12.* https://www.frontiersin.org/articles/10.3389/fpsyg.2021.733554

Garrison, D. R., Anderson, T., & Archer, W. (1999). Critical inquiry in a text-based environment: Computer conferencing in higher education. *The Internet and Higher Education, 2*(2), 87–105. https://doi.org/10.1016/S1096-7516(00)00016-6

Gernsbacher, M. A. (2016). Five tips for improving online discussion boards. *APS Observer, 29.* https://www.psychologicalscience.org/observer/five-tips-for-improving-online-discussion-boards

Gopalan, M., Linden-Carmichael, A., & Lanza, S. (2022). College students' sense of belonging and mental health amidst the COVID-19 pandemic. *The Journal of Adolescent Health, 70*(2), 228–233. https://doi.org/10.1016/j.jadohealth.2021.10.010

Grady, M. (2020, December 17). *The Ever Dreaded Discussion Board – Out of the Box Activities and How to Handle the Workload.* University at Buffalo - Curriculum, Assessment, and Teaching Transformation. https://www.buffalo.edu/catt/blog/cei-blog-121720.html

Jenay, R. (2021, November 5). *EDUCAUSE QuickPoll Results: Flexibility and Equity for Student Success.* Educause Review. https://er.educause.edu/articles/2021/11/educause-quickpoll-results-flexibility-and-equity-for-student-success

Keh, H. T., & Lee, Y. H. (2006). Do reward programs build loyalty for services?: The moderating effect of satisfaction on type and timing of rewards. *Journal of Retailing, 82*(2), 127–136. https://doi.org/10.1016/j.jretai.2006.02.004

Kline, M. (2019). *The Looming Higher Ed Enrollment Cliff.* CUPA-HR. https://www.cupahr.org/issue/feature/higher-ed-enrollment-cliff/

Lane, L. M. (2020, October 14). Why Online Discussion Boards Suck, and What to Do About It. *Medium.* https://lisahistory.medium.com/why-online-discussion-boards-suck-and-what-to-do-about-it-e843a09c16d4

Lempres, D. (2022, May 12). *Is Hybrid Learning Here to Stay in Higher Ed?* EdSurge. https://www.edsurge.com/news/2022-05-12-is-hybrid-learning-here-to-stay-in-higher-ed

Leonard, G. (1992). *Mastery: The Keys to Success and Long-Term Fulfillment*. Plume.

Lieberman, M. (2019, March 27). *Discussion Boards: Valuable? Overused? Discuss.* Inside Higher Ed. https://www.insidehighered.com/digital-learning/article/2019/03/27/new-approaches-discussion-boards-aim-dynamic-online-learning

Lombardo, M. M., & Eichinger, R. W. (1996). *Career Architect Development Planner* (1st ed.). Lominger Limited.

Martin, M. C., Martin, M. J., & Feldstein, A. P. (2017). Using yellowdig in marketing courses: An analysis of individual contributions and social interactions in online classroom communities and their impact on student learning and engagement. *Global Journal of Business Pedagogy, 1*(1), 55–74. https://igbr.org/wp-content/uploads/2017/08/GJBP_Vol_1_No_1_2017.pdf#page=60

Martinez, K. (2019, September 21). *17 Tweets That Perfectly Sum Up College Discussion Board Posts*. BuzzFeed. https://www.buzzfeed.com/kellymartinez/students-on-discussion-board-posts-who-are-honestly-trying

Mazureck, U., & van Hattem, J. (2006). Rewards for safe driving behavior: Influence on following distance and speed. *Transportation Research Record, 1980*(1), 31–38. https://doi.org/10.1177/0361198106198000106

McKenzie, L. (2021, April 27). *Students Want Online Learning Options Post-Pandemic*. Inside Higher Ed.

https://www.insidehighered.com/news/2021/04/27/survey-reveals-positive-outlook-online-instruction-post-pandemic

McLachlan, S. (2022, August 2). Ideal Length of Social Media Posts: A Guide for Every Platform. *Social Media Marketing & Management Dashboard.* https://blog.hootsuite.com/ideal-social-media-post-length/

Okabe-Miyamoto, K., & Lyubomirsky, S. (2021). *Social connection and well-being during COVID-19* (World Happiness Report 2021, pp. 131–152). https://www.researchgate.net/profile/Shun-Wang-31/publication/350511770_World_Happiness_Report_2021/links/6063d797299bf173677dca9b/World-Happiness-Report-2021.pdf#page=133

Okita, S. Y., Bailenson, J., & Schwartz, D. L. (2007). The mere belief of social interaction improves learning. *Proceedings of the Annual Meeting of the Cognitive Science Society, 29*(29). https://escholarship.org/uc/item/7rs81781

Posner, M. I., & Rothbart, M. K. (2014). Attention to learning of school subjects. *Trends in Neuroscience and Education, 3*(1), 14–17. https://doi.org/10.1016/j.tine.2014.02.003

Regular and Substantive Interaction Refresh: Reviewing & Sharing Our Best Interpretation of Current Guidance and Requirements. (2021, August 26). WICHE Cooperative for Educational Technologies. https://wcet.wiche.edu/frontiers/2021/08/26/rsi-refresh-sharing-our-best-interpretation-guidance-requirements/

Reward. (2022). In *Merriam-Webster.com dictionary.* https://www.merriam-webster.com/dictionary/reward

Ryan, R. M., & Deci, E. L. (2020). Intrinsic and extrinsic motivation from a self-determination theory perspective: Definitions, theory, practices, and future directions. *Contemporary Educational Psychology, 61,* 101860. https://doi.org/10.1016/j.cedpsych.2020.101860

Sakulku, J. (2011). The impostor phenomenon. *The Journal of Behavioral Science*, *6*(1), Article 1. https://doi.org/10.14456/ijbs.2011.6

Samson, P. (2022, March 1). *Students Often Prefer In-Person Classes... Until They Don't*. Educause Review. https://er.educause.edu/articles/2022/3/students-often-prefer-in-person-classes-until-they-dont

Smeddinck, J. D., Herrlich, M., Wang, X., Zhang, G., & Malaka, R. (2019). Work hard, play hard: How linking rewards in games to prior exercise performance improves motivation and exercise intensity. *Entertainment Computing*, *29*, 20–30. https://doi.org/10.1016/j.entcom.2018.10.001

Various Authors. (1911). Universities. In H. Chisholm (Ed.), *1911 Encyclopædia Britannica: Vol. Volume 27* (11th ed.). Cambridge University Press; Wikisource. https://en.wikisource.org/wiki/1911_Encyclop%C3%A6dia_Britannica/Universities

Verdine, B. N. (2020, September 24). Why "Discussions" Fail: Reconsidering Online Discussion Best Practices. *Yellowdig*. https://www.yellowdig.co/post/why-discussions-fail

What Makes a Video Game Addictive? (2019, March 15). Video Game Addiction. https://www.video-game-addiction.org/what-makes-games-addictive.html

Yellowdig. (2021a). *Connect Like Never Before* (E-Book Series No. 1; p. 13). Yellowdig. https://explore.yellowdig.co/connect-like-never-before-e-book

Yellowdig. (2021b). *Made for Humans* (E-Book Series No. 2; p. 19). Yellowdig. https://explore.yellowdig.co/made-for-humans-e-book

PART 3

Use Cases of Hybrid

Kimberly Merritt, Elizabeth P. Callaghan, Stephen M. Kosslyn

Introduction: Hybrid in Action

In this third and final section, we move from frameworks to applications, delving into the real-world implementation of hybrid education in various contexts. We hope that our exploration of the theoretical foundations and diverse forms of hybrid education in Parts I and II has offered you not only a foundational understanding of hybrid education but also a dynamic and multifaceted vision of its potential in higher education.

In this section, we provide you with case studies that illustrate the application, challenges, and triumphs of hybrid education. Each case has been carefully chosen to offer a different perspective, from traditional universities embracing the hybrid model to innovative startup programs charting new territory in the hybrid space. These chapters will illustrate the potential for hybrid education to change learning and teaching for the better.

These case studies are far more than just success stories. They are lessons learned from various vantage points of planning, implementing, and assessing hybrid programs. We delve into successes, but we also shed light on challenges and difficulties. By doing so, our aim is to provide an honest and comprehensive portrayal of what it truly means to implement hybrid education. Each chapter provides practical wisdom and actionable insights to apply directly to your hybrid education initiatives.

These applications also illustrate the applicability of hybrid education to different student populations. As we've seen, hybrid education is uniquely poised to reach diverse groups of learners. From underserved populations to adult learners to corporate staff, we explore how hybrid education can cater to and be enriched by these diverse audiences.

Lastly, we project into the future, speculating about the trajectories of hybrid education based on the lessons learned from these case studies and new developments with artificial intelligence. We examine potential trends, burgeoning technologies, and upcoming challenges that might shape the future of hybrid learning.

As we embark on this exploration of "Use Cases of Hybrid," we invite you to keep an open mind. Embrace the complexity, relish the diversity, and, most importantly, consider how these insights can shape your own approach to hybrid education. Let's learn from the past and present to create a future where hybrid education isn't just an option but an inspired choice for transformative learning experiences in higher education.

Chapter 9

Duane Roen

Using the "Available Means": Learning to ~~Write~~ Compose in A New American University

Abstract

This chapter is a case study into the rise and evolution of hybrid learning at Arizona State University, shared through the lens of writing instruction. It will include an overview of innovations in hybrid writing instruction that began in the late 1990s with desktop computers, continues through the journey to online, and then explores how these advances have led to hybrid, community-based solutions that leverage past innovations. The chapter will conclude with a "What's next?" section reflecting the innovations and future experiences that can support hybrid lifelong learning in the next decade and beyond.

"The students of the future will demand the learning support that is appropriate for their situation or context. Nothing more. Nothing less."— Marcus Specht (2009)

The last two decades at Arizona State University have been marked by a strong institutional commitment to innovation that serves students and the community, where "community" is defined as "residents of Planet Earth." As a result, ASU has been named by *U.S. News & World Report* as the most innovative university in the United States for eight consecutive years—and counting. It's important to emphasize that innovation for its own sake is not the goal at Arizona State University; rather, the goal is to innovate so that we can fulfill the pledge that we make to our constituents in the ASU Charter:

ASU is a comprehensive public research university, measured not by whom we exclude but rather by whom we include and how they succeed, advancing research and discovery of public value; and assuming fundamental responsibility for the economic, social, cultural, and overall health of the communities it serves.

Within this institutional context, many forms of innovation across the academic units strive to fulfill the promise made in the ASU Charter (*ASU News*, 2022). Stories of those innovations could fill many books, such as the one in which this chapter appears. This chapter focuses on learning in writing classrooms, something every ASU student experiences. In the title of this chapter, the word *Write* is struck through and replaced with the word *Compose* because 21st-century "writing" courses do not focus only on words on the page or the screen. Instead, they engage students in a full range of tools and methods for expressing meaning. I do use the words *write*, *writer*, and *writing* in places in this chapter, but those words are not meant to imply that the focus is on words only.

A Brief History of the Journey

In the pages that follow, I will describe some ways that we have served students and the community by supporting learners who want and need to compose effectively in all four realms of life: academic (school), professional (the workplace), civic (the community), and personal (everything else). As I do so, I will briefly describe some of my own commitments to hybrid writing instruction, which date back to 1981, and which reflect Aristotle's observation that people should use the tools that are available to them. [In Aristotle's book *Rhetoric*, he defined *rhetoric* as the "available means of persuasion" (1954, p. 24).] By applying Aristotle's observation to twenty-first-century learning—and not just learning to speak and write—teachers have opportunities and responsibilities to guide learners to use all of the tools that are available to them, including the wide array of digital technologies that enrich learning and the application of that learning.

My roles at ASU as a writing teacher, a writing program director, a director of a center for teaching and learning, and as a dean of two colleges—including one that offers student-success programs serving the whole institution—have given me the opportunities to be involved in innovations that support students' learning, especially learning to write. Those innovations in writing instruction date back to the late 1990s, when the Writing Programs at ASU offered some instruction in classrooms that had recently been equipped with desktop computers. Among other things, learning in those classrooms helped students become more proficient in using the digital technologies that were available at the time.

Moving ahead to the mid-2000s, some of my colleagues and I were early adopters of fully online classes, a move that encouraged others at ASU to follow suit. Mostly, these classes were asynchronous, but faculty offered some optional synchronous sessions—both online and in-person. In 2004, I assumed duties as a head of an academic unit that offered courses and degrees in the humanities and social sciences. When the unit offered only on-campus courses in the summer of 2005, a few hundred students enrolled in classes. When I discussed the summer offerings with students the following fall, I learned that many of them had gone home for the summer, with some taking classes at the postsecondary institutions in their hometowns. Because I saw this as a lost opportunity for ASU, in the summer of 2005, colleagues and I offered most of our classes fully online, and more than 1,600 students enrolled in our courses—approximately an 800% increase in enrollment. By the summer of 2006, units in other colleges followed suit.

In 2009, with encouragement from Phil Regier, University Dean for Educational Initiatives and CEO of EdPlus at ASU, the academic unit that I led at the time (now called Leadership and Integrative Studies) was one of the early adopters for offering online degrees—in this case, an undergraduate degree in Interdisciplinary Studies. That degree is offered by the College of Integrative Sciences at ASU, a college in which 4,811 (64%) of its 7,496 students were enrolled in online degree programs in Fall 2021. From the beginning, we have been excited to have opportunities to engage learners whose life situations made it difficult, if not impossible, to complete a degree on campus.

Then in 2011, I led a team that set out to design a "writers' studio" that would replace traditional 25-student sections of first-year composition with a large physical space in which hundreds of students, teachers, mentors, and tutors would be in the space at the same time to engage in teaching and learning. However, some challenges redirected the team to design a fully online asynchronous version of first-year composition ("Writers' Studio"), which now enrolls more than 10,000 learners per year. For the most part, the course sections serve students enrolled in ASU's online degree programs, but there are also sections that meet the needs of students enrolled in degrees offered on ASU's physical campuses. In the courses, students use the digital tools available for composing, researching, responding to peers, and reflecting on learning.

In 2015, under the auspices of EdPlus, ASU launched The Global Freshman Academy, and I was asked to design an open-access version of first-year composition, which enrolled 35,000 learners in the first offering of English 101. In 2021, this and other courses, now managed by Learning Enterprise at ASU, are undergoing substantial revisions to make them function even more effectively to serve the needs of "universal learners"—learners across the span of life.

Of course, in March 2020, everyone teaching and learning in schools at all levels had to adopt new platforms for remote instruction quickly. At ASU, we were able to draw on the years of experience with online learning to support learners who were in on-campus degree programs. It also helped that we had been using Zoom for meetings before the pandemic hit. During the one-week spring break in 2020, all in-person classes were converted to remote learning experiences with Zoom as the primary platform. Of course, there were some challenges. For example, although most faculty members had been using Zoom for virtual synchronous meetings, relatively few had experience teaching synchronously on Zoom. Fortunately, the University Technology Office moved quickly to offer training and technical support. Also, faculty members with the most experience teaching in digital environments stepped up to mentor colleagues with less experience. Across the university, we witnessed many Vygotskian zones of proximal development (Vygotsky, 1978: "the distance between the actual developmental level as determined by independent problem solving and the level of potential development as determined through problem-solving under adult guidance or in collaboration with more capable peers" (p. 86).

Applying What I Have Learned about the Available Means

Because of the aforementioned experiences with online and remote learning and because of what Aristotle taught me about using the "available means," I no longer look at in-person classes the same as I did during the early decades of my career. In addition to the aforementioned journey, in November of 2021, I completed a Quality Matters© certificate in "Improving Your Online Course." The two-week workshop raised my awareness of ways to enhance student learning opportunities in our courses. My perspective now is that in-person classes can be greatly enriched by using common digital tools in online courses. In the next few pages, I will share some examples.

Learning to compose effectively requires learners to engage in the experiences described by several professional organizations in the field. First, the Council of Writing Program Administrators (CWPA), in the "WPA Outcomes Statement for First-Year Composition (3.0)" (2014), recommends that students develop skills and knowledge in four areas: (1) Rhetorical Knowledge; (2) Critical Thinking, Reading, and Composing; (3) Processes; and (4) Knowledge of Conventions. Second, three professional organizations (Council of Writing Program Administrators, National Council of Teachers of English, and National Writing Project) have offered a companion statement, "Framework for Success in Postsecondary Writing," which adds that certain habits of mind help learners to be successful in writing courses and in other settings: curiosity, openness, engagement, creativity, persistence, responsibility, flexibility, and metacognition.

Multimodal Projects

Aristotle's 2400-year-old advice to use the "available means" applies to the modes of communication, the media, and the genres that students can and, I argue, should use in their "writing" projects. That is, we should encourage students to use a range of modes: visual, linguistic, aural, spatial, and gestural. Visual and linguistic are obvious in this context. Spatial includes the ways in which elements are arranged in the project—e.g., the proximity of words and images. However, it can also apply to how elements are arranged in the images that students include in their projects—e.g., photos of classrooms in an analysis of how the arrangement of the classroom encourages certain kinds of interaction. Gestural includes gestures, body language, and facial expressions that help to express, understand, and interpret information. For example, if a student's project includes or wholly consists of video of the student presenting information, the student needs to be aware of how they are using gestures, body language, and facial expressions

We should also encourage students to use the media that are available to them—e.g., word-processed documents, emails, blogs, wikis, digital slides, synchronous chats, websites, posters, flyers, brochures, videos, audio recordings. Further, we can and should encourage students to consider other genres besides the academic essay.

Why should we encourage students to work with a range of modes, media, and genres? First, these communication tools are available—they exist for a reason. We can help students to effectively reach the audiences that matter to them if we offer them opportunities in our classes to use a range of modes, media, and genres. Second, if we want students to thrive in all four realms of life (academic, professional, civic, and personal), we need to offer guided practice in using a range of tools that are commonly used in all four realms. Of course, we should not neglect the academic realm, but that realm does not represent the full spectrum of life.

Shared Google Documents

Among other things, developing and applying rhetorical knowledge means meeting the needs of a diverse range of readers (audiences). A teacher is one member of one audience, so although feedback from an experienced writing teacher can be invaluable, it needs to be complemented by feedback from other readers because one of the biggest challenges less experienced writers face is learning what diverse audiences need from them. Of course, learners' peers can provide much helpful feedback during class, and I devote some time to peer feedback sessions in almost every class meeting. However, as I have learned from my colleagues, we can use some of the available digital tools to provide even more feedback. In particular, for each project in a course, students can do their recursive composing-process work (narrowing topics, generating ideas, conducting research, drafting, revising, and editing) in Google documents.

By sharing their Google documents with everyone in the class, learners benefit from the wide range of feedback the teacher and classmates offer 24 x 7. Other learners in the class also benefit because they see how their classmates are engaging in their projects. Further, they see the kinds of feedback that the instructor is offering. Additionally, the feedback that peers offer classmates helps the instructor see how well students have learned some skills and knowledge sets. Incidentally, my experience of reading peer feedback that peers offer in Google Docs is that students stay more tightly focused on the task at hand when they provide feedback in Google Docs than when they provide feedback in small groups in a physical classroom.

Incidentally, students can be most helpful to their peers if their feedback shows they are interested readers. In addition to encouraging students to offer responses that reinforce skills and knowledge taught in the course, we can encourage them to let the writer know how parts of the project resonated with their life experiences. They can also point out how a language user made a particular rhetorical move—e.g., "You established your ethos by telling us about the training you completed." Perhaps most important, though, is that peers can ask questions that will help the writer understand what additional information readers need. Students can do that as effectively as an instructor can.

Digital Portfolios

Although students apply a range of skills and knowledge when they complete a project, that project represents only a snapshot of what a student has learned in a course. To provide students with opportunities to demonstrate a wider range of skills and knowledge that they have learned, a course learning portfolio is invaluable. In my courses, students begin working on the ePortfolio during the first week of the course and continue working on it every week of the course. The portfolio is not a traditional one that simply collects a student's work. Instead, students use the portfolio to make the argument that they have learned certain skills and knowledge. They draw on their work in the course—as well as their use of language outside the course—to support their claims about learning to use language more effectively. However, to show that they have learned a specific skill or piece of knowledge, they may point to a single image, word, phrase, clause, sentence, or paragraph—e.g., "I used a bar graph to present my data because I wanted readers to easily visualize the sodium content of the four well-known fast-food burgers."

In the ePortfolio, students use the aforementioned WPA outcomes to make the following case:

1. In light of the learning outcomes (demonstrated skills and knowledge) for this course, here is what I have learned:
2. Here is evidence supporting my claims about what I have learned:
3. I think that my evidence is compelling because . . . .
4. After this course, I still need to learn . . . .
5. Here is how I see myself using these skills and knowledge sets in the four realms of my life—academic (school), professional (work), civic (community), personal (friends and family).

The ePortfolio has several benefits for students. First, they have the agency to choose how to represent their learning. By the way, the evidence they offer can come from their experiences outside the course. For example, a learner could describe an interaction with a customer at a place of employment or a scene from a movie or an ad on YouTube. Second, constructing the portfolio is another opportunity to construct a documented argument—a skill that will serve them well throughout their lives. Third, they are speculating about how the knowledge and skills will transfer to other settings. As students consider their learning, they are engaged in the kind of reflection that John Dewey (1933) advocated: "active, persistent and careful consideration of any belief or supposed form of knowledge in the light of the grounds that support it, and further conclusions to which it leads" (p. 9).

In addition to reflecting on the course learning outcomes (the skills and knowledge that students can demonstrate), students also reflect on how they have honed any of the aforementioned habits of mind: curiosity, openness, engagement, creativity, persistence, responsibility, flexibility, and metacognition.

Students construct their portfolios in a platform such as *Digication* or *Google Sites*, in which they can represent their learning not only with words but also with images, voice recordings, video recordings, and design elements. Because many of them craft multimodal projects, they need to represent their learning with more than words.

Students share their emerging portfolios with everyone else in the class so that peers can offer feedback and so that everyone can see the many ways in which their learning can be represented. Thus, the ePortfolio serves as a Vygotskian zone of proximal development (Vygotsky, 1978: "the distance between the actual developmental level as determined by independent problem solving and the level of potential development as determined through problem-solving under adult guidance or in collaboration with more capable peers" (p. 86). That is, as students see peers' emerging portfolios, they see additional ways to represent their learning. Further, as classmates provide feedback on students' emerging portfolios, students see even more ways of representing their learning.

Remote Synchronous (and Asynchronous) Class Participation

When the COVID-19 pandemic disrupted traditional instruction in March 2020, ASU, like most other postsecondary institutions, quickly converted its in-person classes to synchronous remote classes. We chose the Zoom video teleconferencing platform because we had already been using it for other purposes before the pandemic hit. Classes met via Zoom for the remainder of the spring semester and for our 2020 summer sessions. In fall 2020 and spring 2021, we allowed students to meet in classrooms or participate synchronously via Zoom—what we called ASU Sync. However, by fall 2021, students, with a few exceptions, were expected to be in classrooms.

In my fall 2021 in-person section of English 101: First-Year Composition and again in my spring 2022 in-person section of English 102: First-Year Composition, I clearly communicated to students that everyone was expected to attend class in the physical classroom. However, my years of teaching experience told me that students cannot always be in the classroom because of life events—illnesses, family emergencies in other states, flat tires, and more. I encouraged students to let me know if any life events would prevent them from attending class in person. For them, I offered Zoom links for remote synchronous participation in class. I also recorded all the Zoom sessions for students who could not participate synchronously but who could participate asynchronously by watching and responding to the video later. I also realized that some students who attended class in person also watched the videos later because they wanted/needed to engage with the course content multiple times. Students reported that revisiting class meetings helped them enhance their understanding of some rhetorical concepts.

Mindfulness

As the pandemic continued to disrupt people's lives in the fall of 2021, I asked my English 101 and English 102 students whether they might find it helpful to engage in a brief mindfulness exercise to focus our attention at the beginning of our in-person class meeting. In that first activity, we focused our attention on breathing, one of the most commonly used mindfulness activities. After the first time we did that, students requested that we do more activities throughout the semester because they said they helped them relax and focus their attention. We did, and since then, I have provided online resources so that students can easily engage in mindfulness activities whenever they feel the need. Mindfulness is consistent with the course's focus on habits of mind (Council et al., 2014). Many organizations provide descriptions and videos of proven mindfulness activities, including the Mayo Clinic, ASU's Center for Mindfulness, Compassion, and Resilience; the UCLA Mindful Awareness Research Center, and UC Berkeley's Greater Good Science Center. By the way, I have come to appreciate that I experience the benefits of mindfulness exercises as much as students do.

Community Engagement

Because ASU's charter states that we serve not only enrolled students but also the community at large, I feel compelled to include this brief section on learning to compose in community settings. In the last fifteen years, I have offered hundreds of in-person family history and life writing workshops for community groups in the metropolitan Phoenix area. Of course, since March 2020, I have conducted most of the workshops via Zoom.

I have come to appreciate the benefits of conducting community workshops via a video teleconferencing platform: it's convenient for many people; it's an efficient use of time (no commuting required); people from locations outside the Phoenix area, including some outside the United States, are able to participate. Because of these and other benefits, in the future, I will be making Zoom participation an option for as many in-person workshops as possible. I also hope to work with Learning Enterprise at ASU to engage learners on a larger scale.

What's Next?

"What's next?" is a tagline for ASU. I find it inspiring because it reminds us that ASU's ranking as the most innovative university in the United States (*U.S. News & World Report,* 2022) for eight consecutive years is more of a call to action than a label. It inspires us to keep working to discover additional "available means" (Aristotle, 1954, p. 24) to serve students and the community. It reminds us that we can't be complacent. We will continue to seek new tools for serving remote learners, and those tools can also serve the learners who work with us in physical classrooms. We also need to frequently encourage students to explore new "available means" for achieving their goals in college, at work, in the community, and with family and friends.

References

Aristotle. (1954). *Rhetoric*. (F. Solmsen, Ed.). (W. R. Roberts, Trans.). The Modern Library, 1954. (Original work published 367-322 BCE)

ASU Center for Mindfulness, Compassion, and Resilience. (multiple dates). Meditations. https://mindfulnesscenter.asu.edu/meditations

ASU Charter. (n.d.). Arizona State University. https://newamericanuniversity.asu.edu/about/asu-charter-mission-and-goals

ASU News (2022, September 11). ASU named no. 1 in innovation for eighth straight year. https://news.asu.edu/20220911-university-news-asu-no-1-innovation-us-news-world-report-eighth-year

Council of Writing Program Administrators (2014, July), in the WPA outcomes statement for first-year composition (3.0). https://wpacouncil.org/aws/CWPA/pt/sd/news_article/243055/_PARENT/layout_details/false

Council of Writing Program Administrators, National Council of Teachers of English, and National Writing Project. (2011). Framework for success in postsecondary writing. https://wpacouncil.org/aws/cwpa/pt/sd/news_article/242845/_parent/layout_details/false

Dewey, John. (1933). *How we think: A restatement of the relations of reflective thinking to the educative process*. D.C. Heath.

EdPlus. (n.d.). Arizona State University. https://edplus.asu.edu/

Learning Enterprise. (n.d.). Arizona State University. https://learning.asu.edu/

Mayo Clinic. (n.d.). Mindfulness exercises. https://www.mayoclinic.org/healthy-lifestyle/consumer-health/in-depth/mindfulness-exercises/art-20046356

Quality Matters. (n.d.). https://www.qualitymatters.org/

Specht, M. (2009, September 11). Learning in a technology-enhanced world: Context in ubiquitous learning support. [Inaugural address]. Mobile Learning in Context Symposium. Open University. Heerlen, The Netherlands.

UC-Berkeley. (n.d.) Greater Good Science Center. Mindfulness. https://greatergood.berkeley.edu/topic/mindfulness.

UCLA Mindful Awareness Research Center. (n.d.). Free guided meditations. https://www.uclahealth.org/marc/mindful-meditations.

U.S. News & World Report. (2022). Most innovative schools: National universities. https://www.usnews.com/best-colleges/rankings/national-universities/innovative.

Vygotsky, L. S. (1978) *Mind in society: The development of higher psychological processes* (M. Cole, V. John-Steiner, S. Scribner, & E. Souberman Eds.). Harvard University Press. (Original work published 1930-1966)

Chapter 10

Maria Anguiano and Kimberly Merritt

ASU Local: A Case Study of a Community-Based Hybrid College Model

Abstract

This chapter is a case study of ASU's hybrid degree offering, ASU Local. This program, designed to support opportunity youth, combines college, career, and life skills with an aim to increase college persistence and life outcomes. The chapter explains how hybrid learning can bring the community together in attaining this goal, the design of structures leveraged to create the experience, and a review of the early lessons learned.

Committed to expanding access and inclusion within higher education, ASU's hybrid degree offering, ASU Local, has been designed to support students by combining college, community, and career with an aim to increase college persistence and life outcomes. ASU Local is an innovative college program designed by the global research university ASU to bring a bachelor's degree directly to students in their local community. It's focused on cultivating student success through an applied learning curriculum focused on 21st-century learning practices and designed to ensure students have a holistic education that prepares them with creative know-how, habits of success, content knowledge, and life navigation.

As its name implies, ASU "Local" allows students to stay in their local community and pairs in-person coaching and mentorship in a tightly knit community with the flexibility of accessing all coursework online, 24/7, through ASU Online's advanced digital learning platforms. This combination has allowed ASU to create one of the country's first equity-centered college hybrid programs, run by a major R1 research university.

Deconstructing the College Experience

Arizona State University has become the largest, fastest-growing, and most innovative higher education research enterprise in the U.S. The university is guided by its charter, which focuses not on exclusion, elitism, and Industrial Age academic structures, but on inclusion, innovation, and measurable results for students, the nation, and the world. ASU has been named the nation's most innovative university for eight consecutive years by U.S. News & World Report (just ahead of Stanford and MIT). The university's design emphasizes interdisciplinary and transdisciplinary learning and research environments.

ASU's charter clearly articulates that, as a comprehensive public research university, it is "measured not by whom it excludes, but by whom it includes and how they succeed." Previous chapters highlighted the need for institutions to deconstruct the college experience from the core and then rebuild it using an equity lens. Only in this manner can we truly develop a higher education experience that addresses the concerns and challenges of our current learners. ASU Local was birthed from this reconstruction effort, a program built from the ground up to explicitly solve the challenges many potential students face and designed to increase both access and support for these learners.

When we think of a "typical" college student, we often have an image of an 18-24 year old full-time student who is likely still dependent on his or her parents, working less than about 16 hours per week. While this image is continually reinforced in the media, the reality is that only 1 in 4 college students fit that profile.[1] Rather, 75% of the nation's students are what we call "modern" learners. They have a host of responsibilities outside of the classroom, often juggling part-time or full-time employment, home or caretaker duties, and a commute to campus.

---

[1] How to Fix American Higher Ed - The Atlantic

When the ASU Local design team took a step back to identify and reflect on the challenges facing these modern learners, a number of key issues surfaced:

- Students working 20-30 hours
- Navigating the hidden curriculum[2] of unwritten social norms, values, and expectations
- Juggling home responsibilities, work schedules, and coursework
- Rooted in their local community, far away from a "main" campus

Most current higher education structures were designed to serve traditional students. These individuals are often continuing-generation students who are able to live on campus and whose parents have been preparing them for college since childhood. The current system was not designed for our modern learners (often low-income, first-generation, and students of color) who are facing the challenges noted above. Recognizing this disconnect, institutions have tried to develop plug-in programs to offer support through these challenges. While well-intentioned, these stop-gap measures do little to solve the actual design inequities in universities and often leave these learners to find their own paths.

The ASU Local program was designed to solve the core challenges noted above. The move towards a hybrid structure offered much-needed flexibility for working students. That is, the combination of embedding the program into local communities allowed learners to remain rooted in their own community-based support structures while still benefiting from ASU's world-class faculty through online courses taken through the ASU Online program available to them 24/7. While solving for key concerns

---

[2]The term 'hidden curriculum' refers to the unwritten, informal 'rules of the game' that govern the broader college atmosphere beyond the formal curriculum of a student's courses and which may disproportionately affect first-generation students. Examples might include how to converse with faculty, the benefits of office hours, or the importance of internships and networking. We discuss the hidden curriculum at length and examine it from an equity lens in our chapter "The Equity Imperative: Putting Learners' Needs at the Heart of Higher Education Design."

of modern learners, these new design features also challenged the ASU team to consider how to maintain a vibrant, dynamic college experience under these new structures. The team wrestled with questions such as:

- What is truly transformational about time together, either in-person or online?
- How can we create a community without living on campus?
- How can we expand access to career experiences for *all* learners, and what types of experiences would add the most value given schedule constraints?
- How can we explicitly embed the hidden curriculum into the program so learners have one less roadblock?

The remainder of this chapter explores the unique features of ASU Local and explores how it uniquely and intentionally solves many of the inequities within the current higher education framework.

What Does a Hybrid Structure Actually Look Like?

Previous chapters have outlined the benefits of a hybrid degree-offering program. ASU Local applies those benefits with an equity focus, designing a new higher-education framework to address challenges many modern learners face. By identifying and leveraging what is most relevant and valuable in both the online and in-person spaces, ASU Local's intentional hybrid format offers an innovative solution to support not only academic outcomes, such as graduation rates but holistic life outcomes, such as emotional and career support. By designing a structure with an equity lens, ASU Local is redefining and reshaping what a college experience looks and feels like, particularly for modern learners.

ASU Local's hybrid design focuses on three essential C's: College, Community, and Career experiences, intentionally building a program to provide effective, dynamic, tailored support to its learners.

College

ASU has been a leader in online degrees, utilizing innovative, interactive, immersive learning technologies designed to promote student engagement and success. ASU Online has over 300 accredited degree programs with over 60,000 students. ASU Online courses are developed and taught by the same esteemed faculty members who teach on campus, so all students receive the same level of excellent teaching regardless of their modality.

ASU Online's degree program serves as ASU Local's online degree backbone. The online feature of ASU Local's program offers much-needed flexibility for its learners who are no longer tied to rigid course schedules, which often conflict with work schedules and home responsibilities. Having 24/7 access to online asynchronous coursework affords these learners the freedom and ability to design their schedules and their lives as they see fit.

Some may argue that online learners lose out on key components of the college experience or the benefits of in-person pedagogy. Much has been noted in this book regarding the ability of online instruction to pull from the most effective forms of in-person instruction. Thus, the following section outlines the non-academic aspects of the ASU Local model and their significance in student success.

Community

ASU Local creates a hybrid community structure by pairing flexible ASU Online degree programs with carefully designed in-person community experiences at sites close to our learners' homes. In addition to offering an online community of support for tutoring, connection, and coursework, ASU Local has created local learning centers in satellite locations across the country that serve as in-person hubs to augment the digitally delivered content. With locations currently in Los Angeles, Washington, D.C., and Yuma, Arizona, ASU Local brings bachelor's degree options to the communities learners are rooted in.

Each site is a co-working environment in a location with other ASU initiatives, which vary by location. The sites enable students to interact and work alongside other ASU students and professionals and prepare for careers in high-demand job market areas. The sites are also easily accessible by public transportation and in close proximity to diverse employment opportunities.

The learning centers offer an opportunity for learners to build a tightly knit community without having to live on campus. While courses reside completely online, learners are on campus at the learning center two times per week, connecting with other learners as well as their coaches.

In this model, students experience the supportive environment of working with a close group of fellow students. The small-college experience brings learners together with friends and supporters in a caring group designed to help learners excel in the college experience and meet their goals. Just as with learners in a residential campus environment, ASU Local creates opportunities to get together with other students from class to discuss concepts, compare notes, and share strategies.

Coaches

Coaches are an integral component of the ASU Local community experience. A coach's role is multidimensional, simultaneously serving as an advocate, translator, way-finder, and navigator for students in all aspects of life. ASU Local coaches provide unique support to students in a variety of ways. Coaches:

- Look at each student holistically;
- Personally connect one-on-one with each student to understand not only the student's career path but also the broader context in which they are pursuing their degree;
- Connect coursework to real-life events and work situations;
- Build a student's professional network;
- Serve as a one-stop-shop to address a learner's questions;

By building personal connections, coaches begin to understand how a student's outside work schedule, home responsibilities, and other pressures might impact a learner's successful completion of a degree program. By intentionally engaging beyond coursework or academic concerns, coaches assist students in holistically navigating life.

Coaches help to remove roadblocks that many students, particularly those underserved in higher education, face. They help learners find a way forward in the face of obstacles and challenges. The challenges that stop learners from completing their degrees can be big or small: the death of a friend; the loss of a job; a family member's sickness; taking care of a younger sibling; or a difficult breakup. Each of these challenges can cause severe strain on the ability to continue one's education. These events can also come out of nowhere. A student may have two amazing years in a program but see things fall apart in a matter of weeks due to changes in life circumstances.

The coach is there to help a student get back on track. Coaches respond to phone calls and texts and are ready to support at a moment's notice. If a student misses an on-campus session, a coach will immediately check in to provide support as needed. People stumble in life. It is part of the human experience. Unfortunately, these stumbles may disproportionately affect modern learners or those who do not live on campus (Baugh et al., 2019; Joy, 2017). ASU Local has designed a framework such that these learners receive the care and coaching needed to be resilient at these critical life junctures.

Coaches often have a background in both counseling and teaching. This powerful combination allows them to have effective one-on-one conversations to help students progress on their life journeys and manage group sessions with other learners at the learning center.

Each coach supports a cohort of 35 students. This small cohort allows each coach to provide personalized support. Given the limited campus infrastructure at these learning locations, it is critical that the cohort size remains small. Having one advisor to hundreds of students would not work, as the depth and frequency of interactions would be severely limited. With fewer students, coaches can address both academic planning and broader life situations affecting a student's success. Coaches within the ASU Local framework are the main navigators for students at the small ASU Local sites and must have time to provide more robust support.

Career

ASU Local understands the critical role networks and social capital play in landing a job post-graduation. ASU Local also understands that having key experiential opportunities to engage in professional settings before graduation is critical. In this rapidly evolving world economy, a college degree alone is often not sufficient to find that first professional job after graduation.

Research shows that first-generation and low-income graduates have far fewer people in their professional networks for jobs. In other words, their social capital is less than continuing-generation students. In fact, only 30% of first-generation and low-income students who enroll in college each year will graduate and secure a strong job or enter graduate school.[3] These individuals often do not have the professional skills or networks of their traditional counterparts. In fact, they start their career journey with a huge disadvantage in developing networks. For example, even a person's zip code can impact the number of connections on LinkedIn. If an individual is in a zip code with a median income over $100,000, the person is three times more likely to have a stronger network.[4] Just by virtue of where our low-income students live and grow up, they begin several steps behind in terms of landing their first job after graduation (Caspar, 2015; Muskens et al., 2019).

ASU Local understands our students' inherent disadvantages and has built-in curriculum, experiences, and support to level the playing field. ASU Local provides students with a curated, scaffolded series of professional experiences designed to help them define their career path and create a professional network. These experiences include:

- Internships
- Industry mentorships
- Project-based consultancies
- Shadowing opportunities

---

[3] Braven: 2021-2022 School Year • Annual Impact Report (bebraven.org)
[4] Closing the Network Gap | Official LinkedIn Blog

These experiential learning opportunities begin preparing learners for a career in their first year of study and enable students to start building the social capital and professional networks critical in landing a job in their field post-graduation. Students are not merely participating in an internship; they are connecting with professionals that can later serve as advocates in their professional journeys. ASU Local intentionally partners with organizations and professionals that understand the program's vision and are willing to be active role models and mentors to these students as they engage in these applied learning opportunities.

In most traditional campuses, opportunities to engage in career preparatory experiences are only available to a limited number of students. While schools boast of exciting internships available for their students, the reality is that only a minority of students are able to enjoy these experiences. While there are exceptions, for many schools and colleges, these programs are not built for scale or incorporated systematically into every student's experience. Continuing generation students, whose parents understand the importance of these options and can guide their students towards these opportunities, hold a distinct advantage as they don't have to rely on the school to help them acquire these experiences. Further, many of our modern students who work part-time or full-time simply may not have the luxury or ability to take on a long-term unpaid internship.

This discrepancy is why professional experiences are a core part of the ASU Local design, embedded as a part of every student's experience. These experiences are not side or "desert projects" but rather a core part of the holistic programming required for all students. Coaches take a holistic approach to identifying a learner's specific skills and talents. A coach's close contact with students and understanding of the broader context of their learning allows for these experiences to be tailored according to the student's interests and constraints. For example, a student with severe time constraints may join a series of tailored short-term project-based activities rather than a long-term internship. In such cases, a learner may only attend the consultancy a limited number of times, but those visits would be highly curated for maximum effect.

Career connections and experiences bring much-needed job relevance to supplement a student's degree curriculum. Students often need support translating between school and work. The concepts learned in a classroom are brought to life in a consultancy or internship as students test out careers related to their majors and, much earlier in their college journey, determine career fit. The career experiences also help students learn how to function in a professional setting. Basic work functions, such as managing a small project or sending a first work email, can cause anxiety for new graduates. By breaking down the hidden curriculum, ASU Local's career experiences help learners successfully transition into a work environment.

It is also important to remember that exposure alone does not necessarily mean access. If a student does not have the scaffolded exposure and opportunities to believe he/she belongs in a professional space, there is potential for that experience to reinforce those persistent inequities if the manager does not have the time or attention to give to the student. This is why it is critical for ASU Local to partner with organizations that share a common vision and commitment to an equity-minded approach.

To prepare students to comfortably and effectively navigate professional environments, ASU Local builds career skills into the actual curriculum design process, approaching career skills much like we approach developing skills in a traditional subject such as math. Math needs to be explicitly taught and practiced. Professors break down problems into manageable steps, give students a chance to practice, and then correct mistakes. Career skills are no different, and students deeply benefit when they receive similar kinds of instruction and practice while preparing to transition to a professional environment.

To support this development, each week, ASU Local provides required 2-hour upskilling sessions for its students. Topics can range from helping students find and develop their strengths to workshops focused on applying for jobs. Students also participate in 5-7 week-long projects to practice these skills, where they have the opportunity to develop elevator pitches and practice with new audiences, join "lunch and learn" to hear stories from professionals in the field and practice informational interviews with people in their chosen field of study. This type of curriculum removes the opacity of the hidden curriculum. By explicitly embedding career skills into the curriculum, ASU Local can ensure all students are equipped to build and leverage their newly developed social capital and transition into a professional environment with the confidence and internal belief that they belong in that space and have the skills to thrive.

ASU Local approaches every aspect of the 3 C's (College, Community, and Career) with intentionality and an equity mindset. This design process has built a unique program that prepares its students to be master learners, problem solvers, and changemakers who help their communities thrive.

In the ASU Local hybrid design, while the college piece and the academic curriculum are available 24/7 and available online, both the community building and the career pieces are delivered in person. This allows for maximum effectiveness. The program can provide the scheduling flexibility students need while ensuring they have meaningful community and skill-building face-to-ace experiences.

Preparing future leaders and innovators

ASU Local is designed around two impact outcomes, supported by three enablers, to prepare students to become universal learners, capable of learning anything at any time. This approach is vital to our graduates handling uncertainty in a complex and rapidly changing world and making a difference within their communities and beyond. The ASU Local experience is purposely designed to equip students with a robust foundation to be successful in today's accelerated, global, and transdisciplinary world. The table below outlines the distinctive impact outcomes, skill sets, and supporting mindsets and dispositions that distinguish the ASU Local program and its students.

Graduate Impact Outcomes

The graduate impact outcomes are measured by participation throughout ASU Local programming and student surveys. As ASU Local is a young program, these outcomes are aspirational. We anticipate the values, skills, and applications students practice throughout their Hybrid programming will lead to empowering students to transfer these skills to their future endeavors.

- *Changemaking.* Every ASU Local graduate will be able to lead positive change in their communities.
- *Purpose-driven paths.* ASU Local Graduates will know how to create new opportunities for themselves, particularly in ambiguous and uncertain situations.

Enabling Skillsets

- *Wellbeing.* ASU Local Graduates will be empowered to manage their own mental and emotional wellbeing
- *Social connectivity.* ASU Local graduates can build support networks and create life-changing connections
- *Master learning.* ASU Local graduates have "learned how to learn" to future-proof their skills for a rapidly accelerating and changing world.

Table 10.1 Graduate impact outcomes

Graduate impact outcomes	Mindsets & dispositions	Knowledge & skills
Changemaking ASU Local graduates create and lead efforts to effect positive, human-centered change in their local and global communities.	**Embrace interdependence and transformative impact.** • Curiosity and understanding of student's own evolving principles, values, and beliefs. • Deep appreciation and respect for individuals and groups with different cultural principles, beliefs, and values. • Unyielding commitment to improving the quality of life for all mankind.	• Collective Leadership • Cultural Awareness • Verbal/Nonverbal Communication for Leadership • Inquiry Cycles to Innovate/Create • Project Management
Purpose-driven career paths ASU Local graduates strategically select their career path; they remain agile to the evolving needs of their industries.	**Embrace forging new paths and creating new opportunities.** • Vigorous commitment to connecting interests, values, and career path • Agility and flexibility to lead through changing demands of the complex global economy • Self-initiated pursuit of professional development and growth	• Opportunity Wayfinding • Personal Branding • Goal-Setting and Planning • Professionalism • Professional Leadership

Table 10.2 Student enablers

Student enablers	Mindsets & dispositions	Knowledge & skills
Wellbeing	**Embrace their story and the agency it will unlock.**	
ASU Local graduates live well - mentally, emotionally, and physically.	<ul><li>Persistence and commitment to thrive</li><li>Disciplined focus on their north star</li><li>Curiosity for their needs; the tenacity to fulfill them</li></ul>	<ul><li>Physical Health & Wellness</li><li>Financial literacy</li><li>Introspection</li><li>Self-efficacy</li><li>Resource wayfinding</li></ul>
Social connectivity	**Embrace human connection.**	
ASU Local graduates build relationships and networks that foster personal and professional growth.	<ul><li>Empathy to understand</li><li>Authentic care and the pursuit to earn/give trust</li><li>Humility and tolerance to build relationships across difference</li></ul>	<ul><li>Self-Awareness</li><li>Verbal/Nonverbal Communication to Build/Maintain Relationships</li><li>Teamwork & Collaboration</li><li>Listening for Understanding</li><li>Adaptability</li></ul>
Master learning	**Embrace curiosity and the pursuit of learning.**	
ASU Local graduates are lifelong learners; they seek impactful solutions to big and small problems that matter.	<ul><li>Vulnerability and resilience through the stumbles, falls, and triumphs of the learning process</li><li>Boldness to attempt to learn anything, no matter how simple or complex</li><li>Relentless in the quest to understand and learn what we may not understand</li></ul>	<ul><li>Transdisciplinarity</li><li>Systems Thinking</li><li>Inquiry Cycles to Problem Solve</li><li>Time & Task Management</li><li>Digital Fluency</li></ul>

Reducing the capital footprint of higher education

The current higher education system focuses primarily on in-person learning tied to physical classrooms. A major result of this focus is that capital investment and infrastructure have become a limiting factor for growth in many four-year public institutions. The educational delivery models are almost 100% dependent on students in a physical classroom and therefore require an extraordinarily high capital cost per student. Such traditional universities are thus highly capital-intensive due to their reliance on physical learning environments resulting in a prohibitive per-student capital growth cost.

Moreover, with enrollments dropping nationwide, institutions must grapple with the question of whether students even want that traditional model anymore. The COVID-19 pandemic has clearly upended how students think about the value proposition of higher education and what they want their educational experience to be. With university budgets tied to enrollment, institutions will need to pay attention to the shifting landscape, listen to these prospective students and more nimbly adjust what is normally a very slow-moving, and even slower changing, ship.

ASU Local designed its program to meet the needs of the shifting college demographics and achieve scalability without the reliance on large physical infrastructure. ASU Local's hybrid format allows for institutional growth outside of the normal capital constraints. There are real estate and facilities expenses associated with the learning centers, but these costs are insignificant compared to the costs associated with the traditional on-campus infrastructure. The physical space utilized is designed to be highly engaging, vs. passive learning environments like large lecture halls. Further, lower capital costs allow ASU Local to focus on key areas for student success, such as maintaining the 1:35 ratio of coaches to learners.

Importance of Community Partners

In addition to its powerful online curriculum and coaching support, ASU Local needs strong on-the-ground community partnerships to thrive. The program is tailored to local community needs. Community partners bring the important context and understanding of the local area needed to inform the community engagement portion of the ASU Local design. It is critical to deeply understand the strengths and nuances of each community and then design the ASU Local program to best fit each unique community's features.

Each ASU Local site has a community partner to guide these decisions. Partner motivations, focus, and needs may vary, and each learning site will have a unique flavor depending on community needs. However, all partners are united in their desire to see a college design that works for the life circumstances of modern learners in their areas.

Partner Case Study: Arizona Western College

Arizona Western College (AWC), a community college located in Yuma, Arizona, has partnered with ASU Local to bring the program to the local area. Yuma is about a 3-hour drive to ASU's campuses in the Phoenix metro area. AWC recognized the need for expanded educational opportunities to support the economy of the growing region. AWC wanted to increase the number of students transferring to a university but also understood that many students wanted to stay local and, in fact, the region also needed more people with degrees to support local workforce needs.

ASU already had established pathway programs with AWC and a long-standing relationship, allowing initial conversations and planning to proceed rapidly. Senior leaders of both institutions began with exploratory conversations on how best to expand this alliance. ASU already had a presence at AWC, and there appeared to be sufficient demand for growth, yet it was clear that the current offerings were not enough. The ASU Local design provided a way to bring over 100 degree programs to Yuma. It quickly became apparent that the ASU Local design and approach would perfectly fit AWC and the Yuma community.

It was also important to understand AWC's student profile in the design phase. AWC is located near the border and serves a high Latinx and first-generation population, again reinforcing the strong fit with the ASU Local hybrid model. Reflecting both the needs of the partner and the community, the ASU Local Yuma program focuses specifically on a transfer pathway for AWC students.

Table 10.3 ASU Local Yuma Timeline

Month	Activity
November 2020	Exploratory conversations between senior leaders from AWC and ASU
December 2020	Partnership conversations • Transfer of contact data • Recruitment • Financial implications (including scholarships)
January 2021-March 2021	Continued partnership conversations • MOU language • Program marketing • Program facilities
April 2021-June 2021	ASU systems integration to ensure ASU Local Yuma included on all platforms • ASU applications for admission (including transfers) • ASU websites • ASU degree search page
July 2021-August 2021	MOU signed July 1, 2021 Marketing efforts (faculty and staff)
September 2021	Actively recruiting for Spring 2022
November 2021	First ASU Local Yuma staff member (Site Director)
January 2022	Inaugural ASU Local, Yuma cohort (10 students)
September 2022	New Fall cohort (35 students)
January 2023	Anticipated cohort 50-55 students

Under the ASU Local/AWC agreement, AWC provides 900 square feet of facilities space for ASU Local to be on the actual AWC campus. The AWC facilities accommodate both administrative areas and meeting spaces for the program. AWC allowed ASU Local to renovate the space to meet its program specifications. ASU Local completely reimagined the space and brought in the necessary technology. However, ASU Local students are not confined to this dedicated space; they also have access to the AWC campus environment.

While the program is still in its formative years, it is quickly gaining traction at AWC, as evidenced by the expanded Fall 2022 cohort. The program recently brought on its second coach to support the growing number of students.

Conclusion

Solving the inequities outlined in the earlier chapter will not be possible with a passive approach. It requires intentionality, focus, and an explicit willingness to acknowledge and then challenge the existing structures. ASU Local's hybrid program is the result of that intentional, equity-centered approach. This hybrid design purposefully breaks down the structural barriers pervasive in the higher education system that impede the success of our modern learners. The hybrid program reimagines the college experience by leveraging technology and focusing on the most critical aspects of in-person interactions. As the program continues to expand, grow, and evolve, ASU Local leadership remains committed to ensuring that the hybrid program remains true to its equity-centered origins and promotes all students' success.

Chapter 11

Kellie Kreiser

DreamBuilder: A Study in Developing and Modifying Hybrid Training Over Time

Abstract

This chapter examines DreamBuilder, a hybrid women's entrepreneurship program developed by the Thunderbird School of Global Management, as a case study for developing and modifying a hybrid training program over time. Over the decade that the program has been in operation, changes in technology and the abilities of participants have driven the need to modify how it is implemented. The DreamBuilder story demonstrates the cycle of initial planning and design, adapting over time, and reacting to sudden change. This case study examines how deploying different modalities can preserve the effectiveness of a program.

In this chapter, DreamBuilder, a hybrid training program over a decade old that has reached over 205,000 learners, will be used to demonstrate the cycle of initial plan and design, continual adjustments over time, and effective reactions to sudden change.

DreamBuilder: A Hybrid Women's Entrepreneurship Training Program

The Freeport-McMoRan Foundation (Freeport) chose the Thunderbird School of Global Management at ASU (Thunderbird) to develop a signature women's entrepreneurship training program as a centerpiece of their corporate social responsibility program. Freeport selected Thunderbird for its proven proficiency in designing and implementing high-impact women's economic empowerment training programs.(Bullough et al., 2015) These programs leverage the School's expertise in international business education, especially teaching people in emerging and underserved markets how to start and grow small businesses.

Thunderbird develops customized social impact programs delivered on-site, on-location, online, or as a hybrid. The programs succeed in a wide range of formats, from international visitor-style programs on Thunderbird's Arizona campus to in-country training and capacity-building projects, as well as global online programs designed especially for emerging markets. Many projects serve entrepreneurs from developing and emerging economies, with a particular focus on developing female entrepreneurs. Since 2005, more than 260,000 women entrepreneurs from 160 countries have participated in Thunderbird's programs.

Programs are sponsored by corporate partners or funded through grants and delivered by Thunderbird faculty; Thunderbird alumni who live and work in these markets often provide additional support, such as mentoring. Esteemed partners have included the U.S. Department of State, the Small Business Administration, the Inter-American Development Bank, the Freeport-McMoRan Foundation, the Goldman Sachs Foundation, and the United Nations Global Compact Network USA.

In 2012, Freeport contracted Thunderbird to develop a hybrid training program that became DreamBuilder. The program is a free entrepreneurship training program available in English and Spanish. It consists of courses covering the foundational business knowledge needed to start and grow small businesses. Courses such as marketing, pricing, bookkeeping, and others use games, exercises, testimonials from successful entrepreneurs, and video storytelling to make learning enjoyable. A built-in business plan generator guides the participants in creating a personalized, editable business plan. DreamBuilder is available both online and offline. While the program can be viewed on a smartphone, it is best experienced on a computer or tablet.

DreamBuilder was designed keeping the unique needs of women entrepreneurs in mind, but it is used worldwide not only by women but also by men and youth who want to pursue their dreams of business ownership. To date, more than 205,000 people have enrolled in the program, completing over 2 million hours of training. Over 66,387 people have graduated with DreamBuilder certification across 127 countries. Over 100 partner organizations offer DreamBuilder classes and additional support to those enrolled in the program. In the United States, the U.S. Department of State and the Small Business Administration, with its network of Women's Business Centers, are key partners. In 2019, the State Department selected DreamBuilder to be the central curriculum of its "Academy of Women Entrepreneurs" (AWE), a program implemented through US Embassies around the world, supporting women in 89 countries.

Start By Analyzing Goals, Constraints, and Resources

We can reconstruct how DreamBuilder was created in terms of goals, constraints, and resources (cf., other chapters in this volume). The program was initially created to serve women located in Peru and Chile. In countries with mining operations, it is expected (and sometimes required by governments) that the mining companies implement community development projects for the residents who are impacted by mining operations. Many companies operating in the region routinely build infrastructure in these towns, such as schools, hospitals, soccer stadiums, computer centers, etc. While Freeport would often support these kinds of infrastructure projects, they also identified more complex goals and approaches to community development. Instead of simply demonstrating community goodwill, Freeport wanted to alleviate deeper issues, like unemployment, poverty, domestic violence, drug usage, prostitution, and even family abandonment. These social problems were sometimes triggered when workers lost jobs or hours based on variable production requirements of a commodity like copper.

Freeport believed that women's economic empowerment could help achieve their goals of more stable communities, greater economic security within families, and retention of skilled workers who would be available to come back to work when production increased. They saw women's economic empowerment as a route to decrease social problems and ultimately create more economically prosperous communities that would attract even more qualified workers. Helping women become entrepreneurs would create dual-income families that could better weather fluctuations in either spouse's earnings. This financial stability would reduce the stresses that sometimes lead to domestic abuse, drug usage, and abandonment. As well, the kinds of businesses that women often create (such as shops, restaurants, childcare facilities, or guest houses) were the kinds of businesses that made communities more attractive to new workers. Therefore, Freeport aimed to provide free entrepreneurship training for women in the communities where they operated in Chile and Peru.

When Thunderbird was approached to design and implement a women's entrepreneurship training program, the developers used a design thinking approach to develop the hybrid program.

After conducting a needs assessment in the field, Thunderbird identified constraints and resources that would influence the initial design process. Women in the community faced common barriers to starting a business: many had limited education, their literacy levels were varied, and access to capital was inadequate. While many women had mobile phones, data plans were expensive, and they lacked home internet access (and computers). Women also faced a range of demands on their time as they were expected to shoulder the work of the home, childcare, and elder care.

Reliable access to trainers presented another constraint. While many traditional, in-person synchronous training programs had been developed by schools, non-profits, and other mining companies in the past, it was difficult to retain staff for these programs. As soon as someone was hired and trained to run a program, they could immediately leave for a larger city where their newly-acquired skills allowed them to get better-paying jobs.

These barriers formed some of the constraints within which Thunderbird would have to work to create a successful and relevant program. However, there were some bright spots regarding available resources. Years of community development programs by various mining companies had produced well-appointed schools, business centers, and community centers that were often outfitted with computers and internet access. Also, women in these areas were entrepreneurial and hardworking. In both countries, culturally, it was not frowned upon for women to have small businesses, although family demands came first.

After analyzing the various factors underlying goals, constraints, and resources, Thunderbird created an online learning program. The computer centers that had already been built could be utilized, and using an online format would lessen the need for dedicated trainers. Additionally, an online training program would allow women with multiple demands on their time to learn at their own pace.

The program, which became known as "DreamBuilder," was revolutionary in 2012. Not many online learning programs were being created for women in emerging markets, and because of that, few technology partners were willing to work with the School to develop the DreamBuilder program. However, Thunderbird found Bluedrop ISM, a Canadian learning company started by an emigrant from Egypt who believed in the idea, and Bluedrop agreed to work with Thunderbird to develop the asynchronous online program.

Developed to be Approachable

DreamBuilder became a 12-course, lock-step program delivered in Spanish that targeted base-of-the-pyramid women entrepreneurs who wanted to start or grow a small business. The courses were business basics, appropriate for women at the beginning of their entrepreneurial journey. The lack of local qualified teachers led Thunderbird to develop the courses with no requirement for teachers. A fictional character, a female entrepreneur named Alma Florez, "taught" the courses in first-person, sharing personal anecdotes as mini cases. Alma's character was developed keeping in mind that students might lack confidence, be intimidated by computers or math, have limited literacy, and have little to no experience taking an online class before. To address these challenges, Alma was presented as a trusted friend who wanted to help, someone who would share insider information that could help the learner.

The language was conversational, stripped of business jargon. Essential business terms were defined simply. Topics requiring the manipulation of numbers were spread throughout the program in small doses. Even the name, brand, and design of DreamBuilder were constructed to be comfortable, familiar, and encouraging. Creating a business was framed as pursuing a dream. Graphics mimicked bright colors, rounded shapes, and sans serif fonts commonly seen in local food packaging that women were familiar with.

Thunderbird knew that DreamBuilder's target audience had many burdens on their time: the workload at home as well as child and elder care. It would be imperative to develop the program in a way that would accommodate women who could only do a little studying at a time.

DreamBuilder was designed as a set of small chunks. There were 12 courses in the program, each divided into 5 to 7 topics. The program design made sure that the learner always knew how far she was in a course. A course "map" looked like the map of a town, a trope the target audience would be familiar with. A woman icon would walk through the map, where each stop represented the focus of a course. For instance, a bank represented the finance course. As the learner progressed through the courses, each new topic was unlocked. Within a topic, the walking woman icon would move along the topic of the screen, indicating how much more time a learner could expect to spend on each topic. Learners could stop at any point in a course. When they returned, a bookmarking functionality brought them back to the point where they stopped. These design elements were a response to the constraints women faced due to multiple demands on their time. The learner could set her own pace for learning and choose how much time she would spend in the program at a sitting. By informing the learner where she was within an individual topic, in a course, or in the program, she had the information and agency to make that choice.

Thunderbird also understood that people find time to do things they enjoy. Making the training fun and social meant that women would more likely spend precious time on it. Courses were filled with engaging and interactive activities. Thunderbird also filmed a telenovela that was used throughout, with 3-5-minute episodes interspersed through the program. Telenovelas, a popular entertainment format in Latin America, provided the program designers with a resource that drew the women in and kept them from quitting the training. The telenovela told the story of four women entrepreneurs at various stages of building their varied types of businesses. The women characters also portrayed varied relationships with men and children, good and bad. This allowed Thunderbird to show the real impacts that relationships have on women entrepreneurs. The episodic nature (and drama) of the telenovela format also kept the women coming back to see what would happen next.

Another device to encourage course completion was an embedded business plan wizard. Throughout the program, learners were asked questions that led them to apply course concepts to their business idea. Each answer was captured and placed into a business plan template. To generate the resulting business plan draft, the women had to complete the course. Combined with earning a certificate, being able to download their business plan draft encouraged the women to complete the full 25-35-hour program.

However, Thunderbird knew that it was extremely difficult to get learners to complete online courses where there was no real accountability to finish. Normal completion rates of single MOOC-style classes are often less than 5%. Asking women who had significant time constraints and very little experience with online learning to complete a dozen classes representing hours of training was going to be a difficult prospect, no matter how good the program was. While the modality at the heart of DreamBuilder is an asynchronous, online program, Thunderbird recognized the need to also incorporate synchronous, in-person elements through the implementation (and hence relied on a hybrid design).

Therefore, Thunderbird developed DreamBuilder to be delivered by a local partner. Anyone can take the program by going to www.dreambuilder.org but the School decided to create a network of local partners who could offer DreamBuilder. Primary targets for partners were non-profits, schools, and government agencies that already focused on women's economic empowerment. The local partners also had to have access to computers and internet. To encourage local partners to work with us, Thunderbird offered co-branded DreamBuilder landing pages, the ability for partners to collect their own data, additional training and support for implementation, and extra add-ons such as prize money for business plan competitions.

In the more traditional training programs, the partners had operated in the past, they struggled to keep qualified people who could teach. But DreamBuilder made it possible for partners to hire people who could simply be facilitators instead of teachers. The program gave partners a cost-effective way to reach a lot of women and a very professional, branded online program that set them apart when pursuing their own additional grant funding. The structure of DreamBuilder empowered partners to leverage business expertise in the community and to provide local economic context to the program topics by bringing in banks, mentors, government agencies, lawyers, and other stakeholders for extra in-person sessions.

This arrangement gave learners a place to access computers, tablets, and the internet, as well as technical support in navigating their use. DreamBuilder was purposely designed with a simple navigation system, but it was helpful for the women to have someone on hand to help them open an email account and answer technical questions.

For its extensive research and thoughtful design process, DreamBuilder was recognized with a Brandon Hall Excellence Award for innovation in online learning.

Adapt to Thrive and Survive

While the initial thoughtful design of DreamBuilder provided a foundation for long-lasting success in the decade since it was started, much has changed. Over the years, Thunderbird has had to continue to be agile to modify the approach to continue meeting its goal of helping women start and grow small businesses.

Several major shifts have driven programmatic changes to DreamBuilder:
1. Scaling to new places
2. Changes in technology and devices
3. Challenges to connectivity
4. Need for additional content

Scaling to New Places

DreamBuilder was developed first for the Latin American market, primarily for Peru and Chile. With the success of the Spanish version, Freeport asked Thunderbird to develop an English language version so that DreamBuilder was accessible to American communities in the Southwest where the company operates.

The Spanish version had a very Latin American context and style, including the telenovelas. To adapt to an American context, Thunderbird made some specific design and content choices. In Latin America, informal businesses are quite common and allowed. Micro-businesses do not always follow all the rules; for example, many informal businesses do not pay taxes. In the Spanish version of DreamBuilder, taxes, contracts, and other rules were addressed following the cultural context of the region. In the United States, it was imperative to clearly outline what is required in terms of taxes, contracts, certifications, and other legal requirements. This meant adding a 13th course to the English version.

The English version also had different stylistic elements. It was designed with a more angular style and included a diverse array of women from different races. Because soap operas are less culturally relevant in the US, the storytelling elements were modified. Instead of a telenovela, more of a "reality TV" style was used with real women sharing their real stories.

While this new English version was primarily meant for American users located in the southwest where Freeport operates, the company allowed Thunderbird to develop the English version to be also relevant to international users. Thunderbird understood that this program could easily be scaled to other countries when English was made available. As the School developed the content, care was taken to make sure that phrasing and advice would make sense no matter where the course was being viewed. This decision would lay the groundwork for DreamBuilder's future global use.

Over the years, organizations outside of the target communities of Peru, Chile, and the U.S. heard about DreamBuilder and wanted to use the program. Freeport generously allowed anyone, anywhere, to use the program. Thunderbird began signing up and training new partners around the world, including very large partners, such as the Small Business Administration and the U.S. Department of State. The State Department selected DreamBuilder as the core curriculum of their Academy for Women Entrepreneurs program (AWE). Currently, local partners are selected by U.S. Embassies in over 80 countries to run AWE cohorts. The local partners provide additional in-person, synchronous, and asynchronous training to supplement the DreamBuilder curriculum.

Changes in Technology and Devices

When DreamBuilder was originally developed by technology partner Bluedrop ISM, the program was fully coded using Adobe Flash. The program had previously been the industry go-to platform for the kind of interactive online learning used in DreamBuilder. The program allowed synchronization of images and audio in a flexible way. In 2017, Adobe announced that it would be discontinuing Flash. Thankfully, the company gave lengthy notice before shutting down Flash in 2020. However, this shutdown posed a huge problem because DreamBuilder would have to be completely re-coded in a new platform. In 2017, a good alternative was not easily found. Thunderbird worked closely with Freeport and Bluedrop to redevelop the program and shift its many thousands of learners over to the new iteration of the program.

The move had an incredible upside. Flash had not worked on Apple products. During this time, the rise of tablet usage skyrocketed. While DreamBuilder was operable on Android devices and PCs, it could not be accessed on the increasingly more popular iPad tablet. Previously, due to this limitation, program delivery was constrained to PC computers and laptops. With the updated program, DreamBuilder was able to amplify its reach, staying relevant and accessible to many new users who owned tablets rather than laptops. Thunderbird quickly worked with program delivery partners to modify how they set up their "labs" and delivered the program to cohorts of women who could now use the cheaper device.

The change from Flash also opened the possibility of smartphone usage. However, one of the key elements of the DreamBuilder design is the integration of the built-in business plan wizard. That typing-intensive activity requires great effort on a small smartphone. There was extensive deliberation about the benefit of access on smartphones versus the possible loss of this critical design feature of the program. In the end, Thunderbird decided that the benefit of having DreamBuilder graduates complete the program with a business plan in hand outweighed the potential extended reach of a smartphone version.

Challenges to Connectivity

In the decade since DreamBuilder launched, connectivity in developing countries has improved, but in some regions, it is still a major barrier to accessing online courses. Chile and Peru have remained a key geography of focus for DreamBuilder. Freeport has large operations in those countries and a deep commitment to communities near their mines.

In these remote areas, connectivity was not increasing rapidly enough. Thunderbird discovered places that could not be served reliably with the online version when working through local partners. That spurred the creation of an offline version of DreamBuilder.

The offline program looks just like the online version, but it can be loaded onto computers through a thumb drive or downloaded from the cloud. Utilizing the offline version has required Thunderbird to develop additional synchronous activities that are delivered by local partners in the field. The business plan is completed as a Word document or a paper workbook. Tracking participants and graduates must be done by the partner. With these additional requirements, the offline version has allowed DreamBuilder greater reach into underserved indigenous and remote communities.

Another challenge to connectivity was the lack of access to devices. While many local partners have computer labs, women may be unable to travel to these locations. Transportation may not be reliable, safe, or convenient. To address the lack of access to devices, Thunderbird developed the concept of the "Mobile Lab." These labs consist of a set of tablets or laptops, a mobile hotspot, and a human facilitator. The lab facilitator has a regular schedule and location where they set up a temporary classroom. Labs can be held in community centers, churches, government offices, and even marketplaces and parks. The devices are connected online to the internet via the hotspots. Personal progress is recorded in the cloud, so it does not matter which device a learner uses for future sessions.

Mobile labs are scalable, flexible, and affordable. This modality dramatically increases the reach of DreamBuilder into underserved and unconnected communities.

Need for Additional Content

In the early years of DreamBuilder, most modifications were focused on keeping pace with changes in technology. But after a few years of use, it became apparent that additional curriculum could be added to the DreamBuilder program to improve its effectiveness in enabling women to grow their businesses.

The core DreamBuilder program has a module on "Funding Your Dream." While relevant for women in the startup phase, it was not robust enough for women who were ready to seek out more capital.

Thunderbird developed a new stand-alone module called "Financing Your Dream" that provided a deeper explanation of how to access capital. This module was designed as an addition to the core lock-step program. The two-hour course could be taken independently of the core. Here, learners built a "Capital Action Plan" through a similar wizard process as was used for creating a business plan in the main program.

This model of adding stand-alone courses is being replicated with another course entitled "Dream Big." This course is funded through the Women Entrepreneurs Finance Initiative and the Inter-American Development Bank. It focuses on helping women entrepreneurs enter the value chains of other businesses. This development is not only an expansion of the content, but it represents the first-time funding outside Freeport is being used to grow the program. Thunderbird leveraged its relationships with all parties to create an opportunity for mutually beneficial investment in the program.

Working closely and collaboratively with other organizations and local partners to deliver the hybrid elements of DreamBuilder, such as synchronous in-person guest speakers or add-on coaching, has been crucial to its success. The importance of the local partners' capabilities to implement DreamBuilder has become more and more apparent over time. To develop the partners' abilities, as well as their commitment to the program, Thunderbird also created a suite of tools for the partners. These include tools for implementing the program, such as training manuals and videos, best practice case studies, additional resources that could be provided to learners, and an online network for facilitators only. An additional library of video mini-courses called "Knowledge Bursts" was developed to supplement the foundational DreamBuilder lessons. A collection of marketing tools has also been designed to be co-branded. Templates for brochures, signage, promotional flyers/schedules, business cards, folders, and more were developed and provided free of charge. Local partners can also have a co-branded version of the DreamBuilder entrance page. Thunderbird has cultivated a sense of shared ownership of the program. The result is that the partners who use DreamBuilder feel that it is their program and invest heavily in its success in their markets.

Adjustment Over Time

Many of these modifications were planned over time and had long project timelines. Winning approval for the funding of the projects required the School to continually watch for changes in the environment and emerging trends. Thunderbird needed to plan for enough time to gain the funder's approval and complete project development. While these shifts had come slowly over time, in 2020, the pandemic required rapid adoption of new approaches.

React: The Pandemic Arrived

The global Covid-19 pandemic forced a rapid change to the DreamBuilder program. Beyond simply agile thinking, a shift of this magnitude required an almost acrobatic level of thinking. The uncertain and continually shifting nature of the pandemic forced educational programs to change constantly and quickly.

In the case of DreamBuilder, the goal remained largely the same – to help women start and grow small businesses. However, with so many people losing their jobs and so many small businesses experiencing declining sales or closure, the goal of the program expanded to helping businesses restart or pivot to new opportunities. But partner organizations could no longer offer supplemental in-person, synchronous training. Staff that facilitated cohorts that would have met in person were furloughed. Thunderbird's own staff, which usually ran mobile labs or trained partner organizations, were suddenly stuck at home.

However, in many ways, the pandemic also presented a huge opportunity for programmatic growth. The demand (and need) for entrepreneurship training grew. Many people who lost their jobs had to find ways to make their own business opportunities. Those who already had their own ventures often needed to pivot their operations, products, or services to survive. With the increased need for training coupled with the reduction of in-person training programs available, the demand for an online training solution exploded. DreamBuilder participation increased 150% during the pandemic.

Not only did people have time to devote to training with their businesses closed or reduced, but also digital literacy increased dramatically. People very quickly learned how to use video meeting programs like Zoom and Facebook Live. Businesses all over the world also learned how to use online shopping, ordering, and delivery. These innovations opened up the potential for strategy shifts for businesses and implementation changes for training.

During this time, DreamBuilder had to shift from being a hybrid program to being fully online in both synchronous and asynchronous modalities. As well, Thunderbird staff who previously spent most of their time building the capacity of partners became front-line facilitators.

Instead of in-person cohorts, virtual DreamBuilder cohorts were assembled. Paid promotion using social media enabled the team to recruit extensively for these virtual cohorts. Virtual "office hours" were held for entrepreneurs who had specific questions. Recruiting sessions, graduation ceremonies, and business plan competitions were all held virtually. Active WhatsApp groups helped fill the social void and allowed the crowd-sourcing of shared ideas and general support.

With no time to build specialty courses or technology as the School had done in the past, the DreamBuilder staff had to get creative in using existing platforms. Supplemental online synchronous interactions were created to take the place of the normal in-person sessions. The team used Zoom and streamed simultaneously using Facebook Live. DreamBuilder staff developed and ran extensive webinars. In Chile and Peru alone, Thunderbird ran 599 webinars, reaching 38,678 people in two years. Reruns using YouTube, linked to Facebook and other social media, allowed the team to reach more learners asynchronously.

Speed was prioritized over style for these webinars. In some cases, content was developed to be relevant for a limited time. In the past, resources had been spent to develop coursework that could be used over time and for many possible audiences or geographies. In the production of these webinars, content could be very local, such as providing guidance to Native American communities on specific deadline-driven funding opportunities available only to their communities. DreamBuilder staff could react quickly to pandemic-related opportunities with these webinars.

Even with the rapid adoption of digital platforms, there were still issues in some communities. Women who lacked internet or computer devices in the home were unable to get the full benefit of the DreamBuilder program. While the training can be viewed on a smartphone, it was far from an optimum experience to access DreamBuilder on small screens. Zoom and Facebook Live were used to reach these women through webinars. However, one significant issue was the cost of cell phone data outside of the U.S. This cost limited how much training some women were able to access.

Due to the limits on in-person gatherings, Thunderbird suspended the mobile labs. However, as a result, the School began implementing digital "Lending Libraries" that loan out laptops and a hotspot to unconnected women.

Continuing Uncertainty, Constant Agility

The ever-changing nature of Covid-19 continued to cause uncertainty and shifts between totally virtual programming and a more effective hybrid model that includes in-person meetings during the pandemic.

As regions slowly moved out from the absolute lockdown required by Covid-19, some outside gatherings leveraging the mobile labs were possible. It is apparent that some changes forced by Covid-19 will be maintained. Virtual recruiting and office hour sessions remain a boon. And while there is heavy Zoom fatigue, the value of webinars (and on-demand viewing of repeats) is still present. The need to train women on resiliency, pivoting, and dealing with failure also will be a permanent addition to the curriculum.

It remains to be seen whether the demand for online training will continue at the high levels experienced during the pandemic. The desire to interact in person may spur new demand for more traditional in-person, synchronous sessions. However, the pandemic forced a new level of digital literacy onto many in emerging markets that previously had been hesitant to engage in this kind of learning. Online learning is now routine and normalized. For women specifically, online learning may remain a desirable modality because of their multiple time demands and the efficiency of taking training any time, any place. For those women with limited mobility (i.e., those who are not able to drive or be out after dark), online learning may remain preferable.

Lessons Learned
Effective Programs Change

An effective training program doesn't remain static over time. This is especially true for programs that incorporate digital learning in hybrid designs. They depend on technology, equipment, connectivity, and some level of digital literacy. If a program is meant to last, the program designers must be prepared to learn and evolve continually and to keep pace with change to remain relevant, effective, and accessible.

Sometimes, changes will be gradual over time, adapting to the evolution of technology, the changing demand for the skills of the future, new or revised requirements of a funder, and the ever-changing political/financial/social environments that the program lives in. However, changes can also occur rapidly, even violently, due to extreme incidents— for example, a government collapse, a natural disaster, or a global pandemic.

Design Thinking Should Drive Initial Development

A typical approach for developing a course or a program is to weigh the desired program goals, constraints, and resources (e.g., see other chapters in this volume). This is true whether the training is academic or vocational, regardless of the audience. Often, developers engage in design thinking, putting their primary audience at the center of the strategy and solving a human-based problem. They seek the best way to meet the goals of the learner.

However, the program goals consist of more than just the learners' goals, split from the goals of other stakeholders, such as the funder, the government, partner organizations, and the teaching institution itself. Any number of these co-existing goals must be considered and balanced when designing the initial program. For example, consider the varying stakeholder goals of an entrepreneurship training program.

Table 11.1 Example: Program Goals for an Entrepreneurship Training Program

Stakeholder	Program Goals
Learner	<ul><li>Start a small business so that she can provide for her family</li><li>Pursuit of a passion</li><li>Gaining some independence or security</li></ul>
Funder	<ul><li>Building support of local citizens or governments in a target area</li><li>Creating a positive perception to shareholders or other stakeholders</li><li>Developing business opportunities, such as a stronger supply chain</li><li>Cultivating future users/purchasers of their products</li><li>Achieving a mission-based goal</li></ul>
Government	<ul><li>Increasing the economic prosperity of a region</li><li>Increasing the stability of a region</li><li>Making a political statement</li><li>Discouraging a behavior (such as immigration)</li></ul>
Teaching Institution	<ul><li>Expanding into a different geography</li><li>Reinforcing or establishing a brand position in an industry/discipline/learner category</li><li>Achieving a mission-based goal</li><li>Creating a pipeline for future degree learners</li></ul>

Constraints must also be weighed during the design process. The program designer will consider the constraints faced by the learner, the constraints challenging the partners, the constraints of other stakeholders, and the constraints created by the situation. Learners may face barriers such as language, literacy, digital literacy, ability/disability (sight, hearing, mobility, etc.) They may face constraints placed upon them by the nature of who they are – gender, race, religion, sexual orientation. These characteristics may impact the biases they face and limit their freedoms. Individual learners may also lack access to wealth, time, security, reliable transportation, and even support from family/friends.

The Situation May Add Constraints

A learner's situation will also contribute to the constraints they face. External forces include elements such as the legal environment (are they allowed to drive, travel unaccompanied, or participate in a co-ed event), cultural drivers (expected gender or age roles), religion (for example, training programs during Ramadan), geography, connectivity, availability and affordability of technology, reliable electricity, and more. Other situational constraints might include political support and access, the existence of strong local partners, or the presence of organizations that will implement or promote the program.

Another situational constraint related to the individual is how much control the educator has over the learner's time and engagement. A grade school student required to attend school Monday through Friday, from 8:00 am to 3:00 pm, is different than an adult learner in a non-degree program who can opt out of a program at any point.

Design thinking should consider the nuanced goals, constraints, and resources faced when first developing a program. This helps the educator determine the best initial approach to achieve the overall program goals. But as the situation shifts over time, the educator may need to adjust methodology to continue achieving (and exceeding) the goals. This requires shifting to more agile thinking techniques.

Build in Agility to Adapt

A course provider must be prepared that program environments for hybrid learning often shift. Technology, equipment, platforms, and programs may get better, cheaper, and more widely accepted. Access to connectivity and electricity, or improvements of a learner's digital literacy and other skills, may expand the potential audience. As we move further into the Fourth Industrial Revolution, the required skills and knowledge for the future of employment may shift.

Modifications among funding resources, program requirements, new metrics or data requests, competitive forces, and changes in political/economic/social situations can create conditions that will force adaptations. As well, the desire to scale a program into different cultures, geographies, languages, or learner groups will require modifying the program.

In some cases, the measured pace of design thinking's iterative cycle of learning and adapting will be enough. However, although some changes are slow and predictable, others are surprising, unexpected or sudden. Educators may need to be prepared to deploy more agile designing (and redesigning) techniques to modify their programs to keep them relevant and effective.

Conclusions

Reflecting on the more than ten-year journey of DreamBuilder, the arc of "plan, adapt, and react" has illuminated several key takeaways.

- As you are initially designing your hybrid program, can you anticipate what you will face in the "adapt" phase of your program's life? How will you adapt to changes in technology that are sure to come? Although it is unlikely that you will be able to anticipate the future with complete clarity, you know that change will happen. What conversations do you need to have with your funders and other stakeholders in the design phase to make sure that you are aligned on what resources might be necessary if a key platform, program, or technology becomes obsolete? Particularly when your program relies on outside funding, it is important that everyone involved understands that ongoing financial support might be necessary to mitigate the impact of a technology shift.
- Can you build the capacity in your team or organization to be prepared to react to unexpected rapid change? Consider the kind of training your team might require to be ready. This

might include being kept abreast of the newest upcoming technology, bringing up the political/economic/social trends as part of your operational meetings, and exposing your team to the methodologies of both design thinking and agile thinking.

- When you experience a disruption or crisis, don't waste it. What can you learn? What new skills or processes could be repurposed and retained for your program and future programs? In a post-Covid world, reflect on the ways your program may have had to adapt and the ways that you reacted, and think about what you will keep as part of your own methodology moving forward.

Chapter Appendix - DreamBuilder Testimonials

- **Avelina Ccoya (Massage Therapist entrepreneur, Peru)**: "From the very start, from the first classes, DreamBuilder seemed like a game or something. And then, I started associating what I saw and heard with my own story. I always thought I was the only person who had a hard start. I remember saying I should shut this place down; it's not making any money. Then, slowly learning the different topics, and watching the videos, I was really encouraged. And the classroom facilitator who was helping me, she patiently explained what I could not see, which helped me a lot. Now I have a better perspective on how to grow a small business, not only to just pay rent and pay debts but also to take out a percentage of the profits for myself, my own small salary. It was a dream I've had for years, but I didn't know how to start. I felt alone, but today I've started applying the new knowledge I gained from the program."
- **Yanet Coromoto Quintero Hernandez (Owner of Cuentas Araguaney, a children's book company in Chile)**: "DreamBuilder is wonderful. With all I learned, my business has already begun to improve. I liked that technical language is used, but at the same time, it is clear and easy to learn. So much of the information is taught through videos and stories of other entrepreneurs. Through their experiences, I learned a lot. I also liked the idea of the virtual teacher, Alma, because I felt that an expert friend told me what I had to do. The course is well planned, from the simplest concept to the most complicated. And probably the most important part, of course, at the end, you have a business plan ready. Before, this would have seemed impossible."

- **Patricia Robles (Owner of Cocteleria y Amasandería Dayna, a food and beverage catering service in Peru)**: "I am so grateful for DreamBuilder. I was given the opportunity to learn and to open my mind. The program helped me define my business. This is how I was able to realize my dream and move forward. When I started the course, I had nothing. Today, one year later, I'm setting up my own bakery with funds I won through different competitions and with my own savings. I am visible in my community. They know me, and they buy from me. I'm happy with my accomplishments, efforts, and perseverance."
- **Margot Loaiza (Owner of Ventas de Ensaladas Cecilia, a salad delivery service in Peru)**: "The videos in DreamBuilder are very important to the program, as they taught us how to succeed from the start and how to grow our business. In particular, Lucrecia's character in the telenovela helped and inspired me throughout the DreamBuilder program. I was going through a situation similar to Lucrecia's, having problems with my husband, and like her, my business was stalled. This pushed me into a depression. At times, watching videos of Lucrecia, I would begin to cry because I identified fully with her situation, both her relationship with her husband and the business. I walked beside her, step by step, and as her business grew, mine grew too, and the ending to my story was as beautiful as hers. Today my business is good. I am earning money that helps my family. Importantly, I am also emotionally stronger. Today, my relationship with my husband is good. At first, he did not help me or support my work because he did not think it was important. He has completely changed, and now is a pillar supporting my business, helping me to sell and distribute salads in the company van I bought. Now, he respects me and has seen that the whole community recognizes me and appreciates my work."

- **Paris Mock (Owner of Safe Ride Solutions, a personal transportation company in Georgia, U.S.)**: "As a new entrepreneur, I was anxious and overwhelmed with how to start a business. DreamBuilder has been a guide leading me step-by-step on my journey to becoming a business owner. The program has been awesome because it takes the unknown, explains it, and then applies it to a real-life business scenario. Plus, it's very interactive and easy to follow along, helping with the business plan process. I have completed the program, and because of its many tools, I will be able to review any section again to keep me on track for a successful business. DreamBuilder: The best tool for new entrepreneurs and follow-up tool for experienced entrepreneurs!"
- **Blanca Salas Olgado (Owner of Jugos y Desayunos, a restaurant in Peru**: "Before DreamBuilder, I worked on instinct. Ever since I started DreamBuilder, I started thinking about making changes and improving my business. Before, I had never used a computer. I did not think about improving. DreamBuilder helped me to manage a computer and improve the way I work, how to attract clients, improve my store, and above all, how to serve my clients. I now think about opening more stores."
- **Lyndzi Brawley (Owner of the Gila Escape Room, Arizona, U.S.)**: "DreamBuilder helped me prepare for and think about things I had never considered. Even when the course was completed, I have been given many resources to guide my decisions. I may be the sole owner of my business, but I am not alone."
- **Lili Lujan (Owner of La Mamama Bakery, Peru)**: "I was able to buy my oven and start the business I had dreamed of my whole life. Here I am, one year after taking DreamBuilder; I am a different woman! I have achieved my dream. It's right here in my hand. I own my own bakery."

DreamBuilder Screenshots

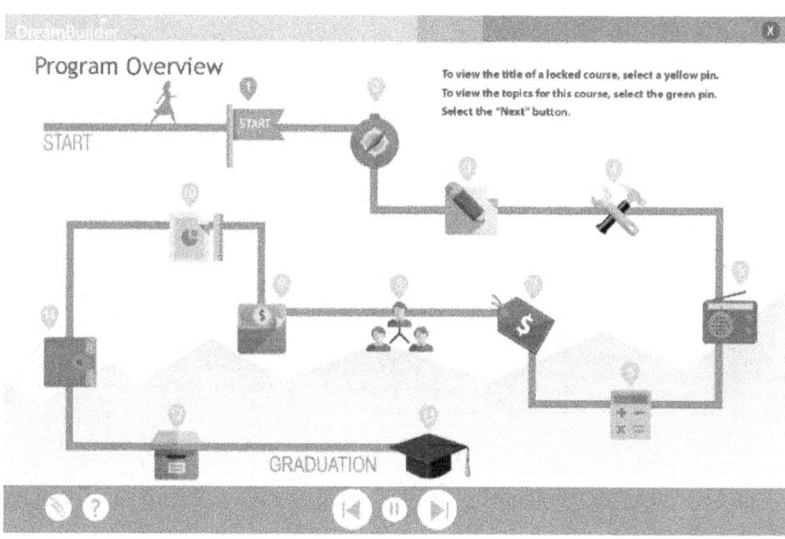

229 | DreamBuilder: A Study in Developing and Modifying Hybrid Training over Time

"Alma," the DreamBuilder narrator, in her pandemic mask

References

Bullough, A., de Luque, M. S., Abdelzaher, D., & Heim, W. (2015). Developing Women Leaders through Entrepreneurship Education and Training. *Academy of Management Perspectives, 29*(2), 250–270. https://doi.org/10.5465/amp.2012.0169

Chapter 12

Meredyth Hendricks & Stuart Rice

Catalyzing Careers with Hybrid Learning

Abstract

Career education, or enterprise learning, has proven crucial for employee retention and corporate competitiveness as the need for reskilling increases due to broad workforce trends. We have learned that hybrid learning combines the benefits of various learning modalities -- remote, in-person, live, and asynchronous -- to provide a dynamic and practical enterprise learning experience. As we evaluate hybrid learning for traits of effectiveness, we discovered the following to be crucial in practice: a learner-centric design approach, a talent strategy focusing on high-priority job skills, and a focus on learning transfer. We also assess the benefits that enterprises gain by partnering with universities, including technical knowledge, new revenue streams, and access to learning design experts to develop successful enterprise learning programs. CareerCatalyst at Arizona State University is offered as a case study with a learner-centric, outcome-driven approach that leverages university resources, including learning design experts, a range of learning modalities, and faculty expertise. CareerCatalyst showcases design thinking principles like learner empathy and emphasizes purpose over product to meet learners' needs. We offer an overview of the CareerCatalyst production process, which works with faculty in the role of subject matter experts to create practical, career-relevant education. The use of such experts and principles allows us to see hybrid learning as a significant catalyst for modern career education.

Advances in technology are changing the United States workforce and in-demand career skills with accelerating speed. The longevity of many technical skills is now 2.5 years or less (Malik, 2020). The implication is clear: All working professionals need to invest in learning throughout their careers to keep their skills fresh and thrive in a quickly evolving workplace.

Hybrid learning works to synthesize distinct learning modalities—asynchronous and synchronous learning, online training, and in-person instruction—in a way that creates benefits unique to their combination. Hybrid learning has enormous potential to deliver scalable, engaging programs that teach professionals skills with immediate applicability and long-term value. Employers, who now widely recognize the potential return on investment of career education for their employees, are increasingly investing in enterprise learning programs in order to transform their talent. Universities, as centers of knowledge and engines of innovation, have leading expertise to teach the workforce critical job skills and competencies. Universities are now working with leading enterprises to improve the potential and impact of career education.

This chapter offers an overview of the rapidly evolving workplace and its implications for skills education, examines the value of hybrid delivery in an organizational setting, and examines the key components of a skills-oriented hybrid enterprise learning program. The chapter also highlights recent hybrid program design innovations and examples of successful enterprise-university partnerships focused on hybrid solutions.

Why Enterprise Learning Is Important: A Macro View

Enterprise learning refers to the learning practices, skills development, and available resources (including finances, personnel, and technology) that enable continuous learning within an organization.

Organizations within any industry or structure may implement enterprise learning, including those in the corporate, non-profit, and government sectors. Employers and employees alike see the benefit of a strategic enterprise approach to continuous learning and development—applying intent not only in the instructional content but the environment, tools, and culture surrounding the learning experience.

While the American workplace has long valued professional development and training, the current environment is actively transforming enterprise learning from a "nice-to-have" to a critical tool for driving employee retention and enterprise competitiveness.

Three broad trends have culminated in an unmatched need and opportunity for enterprise learning:

1. **The Great Resignation:** Employees quit their jobs at a record pace during the COVID-19 pandemic.
2. **The shift to hybrid work:** Many employers are seeing productivity maintained or improved by allowing a balance of on-site and remote work.
3. **Upskilling momentum:** People in the workforce have recognized the growing need to upskill and increasingly diverse and relevant learning options available to develop new and existing skill sets.

The COVID-19 pandemic created a structural shift in the U.S. workforce, resulting in many American workers rethinking their relationship to work. High voluntary resignation rates deeply impacted industry, causing acute talent shortages and making talent acquisition increasingly difficult. A record-high 47.8 million American workers quit their jobs in 2021, with monthly counts trending upward over time. Roughly 3.3 million workers quit in the first month of the year, peaking at over 4.5 million in November 2021 (Interactive Chart: How Historic Has the Great Resignation Been? 2022). Top reasons workers cited for quitting included low pay, limited schedule flexibility, and lack of advancement opportunities, childcare, and benefits (Flynn, 2022). Many Americans re-evaluated their priorities in the face of the pandemic, and the feelings of being underpaid and undervalued motivated many to switch jobs or leave the workforce altogether.

For increased safety during the peak of the COVID-19 pandemic, the U.S. workforce embraced greater integration of remote work. According to Gallup, around 60 million people—half the full-time American workforce—claim to be "remote-capable employees." As such, their work scope includes tasks they can accomplish remotely during all or a portion of the work week (Wigert & Pendell, 2022). Remote-capable employees surveyed by Gallup reported that they expect a hybrid work schedule to become the predominant office arrangement soon, with about 53% expecting a hybrid arrangement and 24% expecting to work remotely exclusively. With many leaders and employees preferring a hybrid arrangement that balances in-office time and remote work, enterprise leaders have now identified the challenge of cultivating a positive, engaging, and cohesive culture with a new model of hybrid employee engagement. With an increasingly hybrid workforce in which employees may be geographically dispersed, organizations have had to adapt employee learning to include both in-person and remote employees. Hybrid learning options can meet this need. In addition, organizations have also seen hybrid learning as a means to create an engaging and cohesive culture with a hybrid workforce.

As many U.S. workplaces move to a hybrid model of work, accelerating automation and digitalization are quickly changing the nature and quantity of available jobs. One pessimistic view of the future is that this transformation of jobs will displace millions of workers with outdated skills. Yet, there remains reason for optimism: The World Economic Forum estimates that by 2025, technological advancement will create at least 12 million more jobs than it destroys (Nunes, 2021). If enterprise leaders partner with education providers, governments, and other key stakeholders to prepare learners for these roles, accelerating automation has the potential to become a net positive for industry, learners, and society as a whole.

Learners and employers recognize the broad need and opportunity for reskilling. According to a PwC survey of 32,500 workers, 77% report being ready to learn new skills or completely retrain (*Upskilling Hopes and Fears 2021*, n.d.). Moreover, eighty percent of CEOs consider teaching their workforce new skills to be their biggest business challenge (Reuveni, 2021).

These tectonic shifts in the value of continuous learning have motivated employers to invest in enterprise learning and spurred innovations to support the delivery of high-impact programs.

The Business Case for Investment in Enterprise Learning

Enterprise learning allows an organization to invest in its employees and, ultimately, its bottom line. There are many benefits of enterprise learning from the ***enterprise perspective***:

- *The financial bottom line.* Most employers now accept that it is typically less expensive to reskill or educate a current employee for an in-demand role compared to hiring external talent (*2022 Workplace Learning Report: The Transformation of L&D*, n.d.). The financial picture varies based on context, but the business case is clear: Replacing a salaried employee can cost 6–9 months of their salary, including recruitment costs (including direct talent acquisition costs and the time for employees involved in the hiring process), onboarding costs, and lost productivity as the new employee gets up to speed (Charaba, 2022). Reskilling current employees often costs $10,000 or less per employee in direct training costs, plus the time for the employee to invest in learning. Enterprise leaders can conduct a targeted assessment of the return on investment for learning programs by assessing the cost of reskilling vs. hiring for in-demand roles.

- *Employee value and engagement.* The availability of enterprise learning signals that an organization highly values employees' education, skills, and advancement. Providing enterprise learning shows employees that the organization is invested in them and directly addresses the grievances of people leaving their current workplaces (as noted above). When employees feel that their employer has invested in their development, they will, in turn, increasingly invest in their work. This improved engagement shows up in improved employee retention: Companies that focus on enterprise learning and internal mobility retain employees for an average of 5.4 years versus the industry average of 2.9

years (*Where Internal Mobility Is Most Common since COVID-19: Top Countries, Industries, and Jobs*, 2020).
- **Culture.** According to Glint Data, work cultures that actively promote "opportunities to learn and grow" can drive retention, engagement, and employee satisfaction (*Employee Well-Being Report*, 2021). Enterprise learning can foster a shared culture and language among employees—regardless of whether they work in person or remotely—as they engage in learning together.

Changing Landscape of Enterprise Learning—Evolving to a Hybrid Approach

As the need for enterprise learning has increased, the enterprise learning "toolbox" has developed significantly. As many organizations have moved to remote work, they have adopted new technologies and tools to enable remote communication and collaboration. Virtual conferencing technology such as Zoom became the primary tool for meetings during the lockdown and has since been integrated into ongoing work. As the pandemic led to the widespread closure of schools and universities, educators also needed new technologies to support remote learning. This shift led to a rapid acceleration of investment and innovation in education technology.

Many of these newly developed tools facilitate hybrid learning models. Corporate training once focused on live, in-person instruction *or* individual, asynchronous computer-based training. In contrast, technology-enabled hybrid learning models, such as synchronous online training or self-paced online courses that end with an in-person capstone, now allow for a more dynamic learning experience that promotes learner skill development while enriching organizational culture.

From content libraries such as LinkedIn Learning to custom-developed programs that leverage frontier technologies, the number of learning options available to organizations has increased significantly compared to pre-pandemic offerings. Select examples of high-impact innovations and tools changing the enterprise education landscape include the following:

Table 12.1 Innovations and Tools Changing the Enterprise Learning Landscape

Innovations	Description
Synchronous Learning Platforms	Synchronous learning platforms enable real-time interaction in a virtual setting among learners and instructors. Examples: Zoom, Engageli
Data and Analytics Capabilities	Virtual and online platforms for learning offer a range of data and analytics capabilities in critical areas such as learner engagement (e.g., talk time or time spent reviewing course materials), progress, and outcomes. Data and analytics can enable the facilitation of enhanced learning and transfer. For example, data and analytics can identify areas where learners need additional assistance or opportunities for targeted interventions, such as personalized feedback or coaching. Emerging tools also allow for an individualized approach to training in which artificial intelligence adapts content delivery to meet an employee's unique training needs. Data and analytics also allow enterprises to calculate the return on investment of their learning programs, which helps them plan strategically to maximize the impact of their training resources. Examples: Hubspot, Google Analytics, Canvas
Learning Content Platforms	Learning content platforms offer skills education content from a variety of sources, including top universities and organizations. Enterprises can rapidly deploy such platforms for employee learning and development. Learning content platforms have evolved to support a variety of learning experiences, from asynchronous "micro-learning" to synchronous, multi-month boot camps. Examples: Coursera, edX, Udemy business
Virtual Reality and Augmented Reality	Virtual Reality (VR) is a computer-generated environment, most frequently perceived through a VR headset, which immerses learners in virtual surroundings. Augmented Reality (AR) combines real-world and computer-generated content by

| | superimposing a computer-generated image on a user's real world view.

By exposing learners to environments that might otherwise be costly or dangerous to access, VR and AR have tremendous potential to advance skills education. When deployed effectively, benefits can include improving learner engagement, increasing empathy, and improving transfer of skills.

Examples: Dynepic, CenarioVR, Dreamscape Learn |
|---|---|

Note. The table shows examples of high-impact changes to corporate education as an industry.

With the ubiquity of tools that facilitate remote engagement, enterprise leaders must balance the benefits and trade-offs of in-person and online approaches when designing enterprise learning programs—several benefits of in-person interaction that are near-impossible to replicate remotely. Notable benefits include improved collaboration, morale, and other features of team culture (Mancl & Fraser, 2022). Information is more readily accessible, and miscommunications are more easily addressed when coworkers are only a desk visit away. The same can be said for in-person learning outcomes, many of which are impossible to accomplish in remote-only environments, such as the many physical skills that require hands-on practice. For example, many types of engineering jobs—mechanical engineering, electrical engineering, and aerospace engineering—require a combination of physical and intellectual work. The manual work of engaging with machinery and equipment is best suited to in-person training, while the academic and intellectual skills can be learned online.

In-person learning provides the opportunity for more immediacy and naturalism in the learning setting: to raise specific questions with immediate answers—and without communication barriers, practice newly gained knowledge through hands-on experience, and even receive instantaneous feedback on the application of newly learned skills. Online learning has its own benefits—greater ability to scale, easily recorded and redeployed later, and simplified tracking of employee completion and performance—that employers can't ignore, but carefully designed hybrid learning can serve to amplify the strengths and compensate for the weaknesses of in-person and remote learning, respectively. With options expanding and technology advancing, organizations must determine which learning approach will maximize learning outcomes within their local setting and organizational culture.

Example

An engineering company is looking to train employees on effective preparation before entering a clean room. The company reviews various options, including on-site training, hybrid training, and fully VR-based experience. As they consider the tradeoffs, they note that on-site training will provide high fidelity but has costs related to bringing people on-site. While VR looks attractive as a model, they discuss that building the VR course will take time and are unsure of what will happen if the training needs to be updated (particularly if protocols and equipment change). Their hybrid option would consist of pre-training online, followed by in-person training.

This chapter defines "hybrid learning" as learning that leverages a combination of more than one learning modality, including asynchronous and synchronous learning. Examples of workplace learning methods and modalities are summarized below. (Please refer to Chapter 4 for an alternative version of this table.)

Table 12.2 Common Workplace Learning Methods Within Learning Modalities

In the workplace	Asynchronous	Synchronous
In-Person	• Independent review of learning materials • Independent practice with skills	• Classroom training on new techniques • On-the-job training • Skills brush up with a more experienced professional
Online	• On-demand course content	• Live webinars with Q&A

	• Recorded webinars	• Group Sessions held via videoconferencing • Telephone discussions with a colleague or colleagues

Note. The table lists asynchronous and synchronous learning options offered online and in person.

As employees in "white-collar" jobs move to more hybrid work, hybrid professional development becomes a natural extension of that environment. While employees embrace hybrid and remote work, they remain concerned about career advancement and gaining the skills necessary to stand out among their colleagues. These worries become particularly salient when managers have less freedom to observe employees doing their work. Hybrid training can provide employees with new skills as well as opportunities to demonstrate proficiency and interest in advancement to their employers.

The benefits of enterprise learning from the ***employee perspective*** focus on practical considerations along with positive social engagement. Practically, employees benefit from the flexibility to fit asynchronous training into their schedules without interfering with professional or personal commitments. Synchronous training components encourage the required connectedness with fellow employees, managers, and organizational leaders to increase the fidelity and contextualization of training. Connectedness allows training to become an emotional investment, enhancing the transfer of learning. Employees are also markedly better at implementing training when they learn skills in a work context—especially because training with synchronous components allows for immediate feedback in context.

For employees in frontline service jobs, such as retail or customer care representatives, hybrid learning can be an effective way to gain advancement through skill acquisition. Asynchronous training modules can provide short-duration, focused training sessions that improve existing skills and add new ones. As employees may be balancing multiple priorities, these asynchronous modules ideally provide practical skills rather than focus on the theory of practice.

Example

A large food service organization wanted to enhance the general career skills of their employees. To do so, they turned to ASU CareerCatalyst for potential solutions. A key requirement was that employees be able to take training both on and off the clock and in a mobile-friendly way. One approach that we recommended was the Professional Skills for Everyone series. This series provides learners with short learning sequences (about 4–6 minutes) and activities to strengthen in-demand professional skills, all available on mobile devices. By implementing this solution, employees were able to improve their skills with minimal time investment, adding immediate value to the company and increasing their opportunities for promotion inside the organization.

While effective as a standalone offering, asynchronous skills training can benefit from additional organizational, managerial, and leadership support, which all come from the synchronous hybridization discussed more below. For example, we know that employees need (a) the opportunity to practice their skills; (b) feedback on their performance from managers or leadership; and (c) positive reinforcement and recognition for their skills.

Keeping this in mind, we would add to our example above. To maximize training benefits, managers would know what skills employees recently learned. Then, these managers would actively provide opportunities for employees to practice these skills and provide feedback that reinforces a growth mindset and the potential for improvement. In addition, the manager or organization would recognize employees who had participated in the skills development training. These factors improve the implementation of learned skills and encourage others to pursue training opportunities.

The Qualities of Effective Hybrid Learning in an Enterprise

To be most effective, enterprise learning should be driven by a talent development strategy emphasizing the training of job-relevant skills that the existing workforce can readily apply. High-impact enterprise learning programs can address the learning needs of employees in any role or at any level—from marketing to operations, frontline staff to executive leadership—by leveraging different permutations of hybrid learning. Organizations should design enterprise learning to focus on high-priority job skills and capabilities that align with the learning opportunities for a specific audience of employees. Those designs should deliver learning according to how that audience will most effectively learn those skills. Enterprise leaders can collaborate with learning design experts to assess the optimal delivery approach for each unique circumstance.

A comprehensive review of effective learning design practices in enterprise learning and development (L&D) is beyond the scope of this chapter. However, L&D leaders and staff must recognize the important qualities that maximize the transfer of training into the workplace. Without this transfer, corporate L&D programs risk wasting thousands of hours of employee time—and millions of dollars—with ineffective approaches. Fortunately, there are a small number of dimensional qualities that the research and practical literature highlight as important for successful transfer (Tonhäuser & Büker, 2016, 147–150).[5]

---

[5] For readers interested in deeper investigation of these topics, we recommend Baldwin and Ford's seminal 1988 article "Transfer of training: A review and directions for future research" with any of the thousand and more articles citing their work. For a more recent literature review, we recommend Tonhauser and Buker's 2016 article "Determinants of Transfer of Training: A Comprehensive Literature Review."

Table 12. 3 Qualities to Facilitate Successful Learning Transfer

Workplace	Instructional Material	Individual
• Opportunities to use training • Social and managerial support for learning • Positive and negative consequences of implementing training	• Content and focus of training • Application and implementation of learning design principles	• Cognitive skills • Prior knowledge • Motivation to transfer learning • Other personal factors

Note. The table identifies qualities of training material, environment, and participants that contribute to successful learning transfer.

Workplace transfer of training research focuses on three areas: workplace factors, the content and design of learning, and personal factors of employees. Personal factors could include employee self-efficacy, intrinsic motivation to learn, and openness to gaining new knowledge and technical skills. For employees in this category, L&D professionals should strive to design learning environments that reduce friction for these highly motivated employees to participate in and complete training sessions.

In hybrid training, qualities of such an environment can mean allowing trainees to work ahead, extending recognition, and providing opportunities to assist fellow employees. Working ahead might not even be possible in most traditional in-person training, but hybrid learning allows for components that actively encourage the practice. In strictly online settings, learners often don't get to work with others; hybrid models make this possible, even when content is partially online. Hybrid training experiences provide an excellent opportunity to elicit immediate feedback and input from employees with lower intrinsic motivation, making interactions and observations that will help the trainer learn what support is needed.

However, even the most motivated employees will find it difficult to transfer training in a poorly designed workplace environment.

Consequently, extant literature also highlights the need for certain workplace factors. Key qualities of this kind include:

- **Opportunities to practice learned skills.** The most important condition is that employees have the ability to practice their skills. Newly learned skills will decay without practice, so intentionally providing opportunities for employees to use their skills is essential. This necessity is true for any form of training, including hybrid modalities. Hybrid-specific skills (like hosting a blended learning presentation with both live and remote attendees) may require specific opportunities prepared ahead of time by the presenter or organization. Hybrid training also allows skills to be tested and applied in varied contexts, a consistent hallmark of general learning transfer principles.
- **Supervisor support and feedback.** Supervisors need to give newly trained employees feedback on their performance of skills. Organizations make a critical mistake when they assume that training alone is enough for skill mastery. In cases of hybrid learning, supervisors may need to provide preplanned opportunities for observation and feedback. Such feedback may include (but isn't limited to) correction, thoughtful prompts, and questions, or even a moment to communicate the underlying principles of the learning objective. Having such useful references on-hand (a benefit of online learning) can't be outweighed by the benefit of having immediate feedback in synchronous training environments.
- **Positive organizational environment.** This environment regards a broad category of conditions. However, research proves that employees and employers benefit from an environment that supports development (Baldwin, Ford, & Bloom, 2009). Building in features like recognition for employees, including advancement opportunities, are an important element that supports the transfer of learning into

the workplace. Such rewarding, encouraging settings are also conducive to "self-prompting," as learners become more encouraged to look on their own for opportunities to absorb the information they need in different contexts.

This list is not exhaustive, but it highlights important elements. In the cases of hybrid training and hybrid work environments, the key takeaway is a level of *intentionality* around employee support after training takes place. Online learning components allow for various enhanced training tools and increased flexibility, but failure to be intentional about training follow-up can lead to lost benefits of training and employee dissatisfaction. This is especially true of skills learned in an online context. Leveraging such intentional training design—specifically that follow-up—requires an employer to address the previous factors listed. An organization can achieve this kind of success in learning design by discovering the unique portfolio of benefits offered in hybrid learning.

Benefits of Hybrid Enterprise Learning

As workplaces transform through increased automation and digitalization, they will recognize the distinct benefits of hybrid learning models. At the same time, hybrid learning must distinguish itself from traditional "one-size-fits-all" approaches of in-person training and the sometimes-debilitating disconnect in online-only learning models.

Enterprise learning with a hybrid delivery carries the respective benefits of both online and in-person learning environments. For example, hybrid learning offers the chance to give center stage to distinct components of the learning experience. Online training can focus on content about knowledge and skills varying in relevant depth, while in-person instruction instills practical use of those skills and their cultural impact.

In other words, online learning more narrowly focuses learner attention and bolsters understanding of skills at levels that sometimes can't be replicated in person. In-person learning provides the opportunity to apply those skills in their specific professional contexts with greater fidelity and less distance between practice and application. Learning how to do something like leading a meeting in an online course creates a flawed context compared to running a meeting complete with personnel and a physical setting. Leveraging the individual strengths of these respective environments creates a comprehensive learning experience greater than the sum of its parts.

Other clear benefits of this hybrid learning model exist, including how it mirrors the professional life of the post-pandemic workforce. Work has, in many cases, become increasingly digital, with technology both preserving and enhancing many human elements of business operations. Hybrid delivery also promotes efficient reuse and redeployment of existing learning assets, transforming in-person sessions into videos or using online responses to stoke live conversations about training material. The use of hybrid learning also creates a far more flexible learning experience. While online learning provides time flexibility for the individual, the in-person components allow people to make the most of their interaction with an instructor. Such interactions, along with the data gathered from online sessions, even help to increase the quality of the learning experience. A distinctly learner-centric approach is possible when combining these two components, as in-person learning expands on the skills from online training.

In 2021, money spent on training programs, materials, and experts reached $92.3 billion—nearly $10 billion more than the previous year. This increasing investment contributes to high stakes and higher expectations, producing frustration due to mixed results. Successful training demonstrates a transfer of learning from theory to practice. Hybrid designs in enterprise learning offer unique benefits to facilitate that transfer. According to Grossman and Salas (2011), the benefits of hybrid delivery include enhancing the following three key factors that affect learning transfer.

- *Transfer climate.* This refers to the environment an organization creates to reinforce training outcomes. A positive learning transfer climate comprises managers who integrate newly-learned skills into the work environment and coworkers who recognize these efforts from one another. Hybrid learning contributes to positive transfer climates by providing distinct opportunities for learning, recognition, and integration of new knowledge and skills. Hybrid learning models also facilitate self-reinforcement through the on-demand availability of reference materials and interactive learning activities.

- *Opportunities to perform.* Successful transfer of learning requires the commitment of learning outcomes to long-term memory. When training allows learners to apply their newfound knowledge and skills, they actively commit that information to long-term memory. Hybrid enterprise learning uses hands-on training to contextualize information and reinforce its practical, productive application.
- *Training follow-up.* Much like the previous factors, the follow-up to training can include support from management and opportunities to test new knowledge and skills. Hybrid training models can create follow-up actions that feel integral to both in-person and online learning processes: these include a review of training impact, additional training options, and personal recognition.

Technology alone can improve fidelity in this transfer process, but research shows that training benefits greatly from the conditions of real-world context. Considering both of these components reveals hybrid delivery as an incredibly useful tool for enterprise learning and development goals.

Cross-Sector Collaboration around Enterprise Learning

Industry-wide, it's typical for learning and development experts or consultants to spearhead enterprise learning by designing, developing, and facilitating training programs. Emerging technologies within a hybrid learning environment now also open opportunities for enterprises to partner with universities to redefine career education and utilize the deep technical knowledge available in higher education.

Faculty live and breathe in the education landscape. Applying an education lens within an industry context allows faculty to engage beyond enrolled students and connect with enterprise employees. Leading faculty members are often active or former practitioners and subject matter experts in technical areas, able to bring their deep knowledge and experience to a corporate setting. In this way, enterprise employees receive training from some of the best minds in the country, and tenure and non-tenure faculty members are able to increase their profiles and possibly receive stipends for new training developments or course facilitation.

In a time of declining university enrollments across the country, partnerships with enterprises afford new revenue streams to universities outside of enrolled students. This change in the revenue model can create win-win situations for universities and enterprises alike.

Translating Academic Approaches to Enterprise Learning

Designing effective skills-education programs for enterprise learners requires a distinctly different approach compared to the design of traditional academic programs. Within higher education, individual faculty members are generally the gatekeepers of knowledge for students. Student outcomes are taken into account during the initial phases of course design, but academic coursework is, first and foremost, a vehicle for knowledge acquisition (learning new facts and concepts). Accordingly, future iteration tends to focus solely on refining structure and content. Enterprise learning places a greater emphasis on skill acquisition (learning to perform a task or activity) and produces developments focused on improving applicability and outcomes. Designing a training program for an enterprise team requires a nuanced approach with a keen understanding of the learner's goals, constraints, and overall work context. Faculty are often ill-equipped to design training programs that align with the skills education needs of specific audiences of working learners.

Because of this disconnect, universities must seek out an intermediary to translate faculty knowledge into practical training for an

coworkers who recognize these efforts from one another. Hybrid learning contributes to positive transfer climates by providing distinct opportunities for learning, recognition, and integration of new knowledge and skills. Hybrid learning models also facilitate self-reinforcement through the on-demand availability of reference materials and interactive learning activities.
- *Opportunities to perform.* Successful transfer of learning requires the commitment of learning outcomes to long-term memory. When training allows learners to apply their newfound knowledge and skills, they actively commit that information to long-term memory. Hybrid enterprise learning uses hands-on training to contextualize information and reinforce its practical, productive application.
- *Training follow-up.* Much like the previous factors, the follow-up to training can include support from management and opportunities to test new knowledge and skills. Hybrid training models can create follow-up actions that feel integral to both in-person and online learning processes: these include a review of training impact, additional training options, and personal recognition.

Technology alone can improve fidelity in this transfer process, but research shows that training benefits greatly from the conditions of real-world context. Considering both of these components reveals hybrid delivery as an incredibly useful tool for enterprise learning and development goals.

Cross-Sector Collaboration around Enterprise Learning

Industry-wide, it's typical for learning and development experts or consultants to spearhead enterprise learning by designing, developing, and facilitating training programs. Emerging technologies within a hybrid learning environment now also open opportunities for enterprises to partner with universities to redefine career education and utilize the deep technical knowledge available in higher education.

Faculty live and breathe in the education landscape. Applying an education lens within an industry context allows faculty to engage beyond enrolled students and connect with enterprise employees. Leading faculty members are often active or former practitioners and subject matter experts in technical areas, able to bring their deep knowledge and experience to a corporate setting. In this way, enterprise employees receive training from some of the best minds in the country, and tenure and non-tenure faculty members are able to increase their profiles and possibly receive stipends for new training developments or course facilitation.

In a time of declining university enrollments across the country, partnerships with enterprises afford new revenue streams to universities outside of enrolled students. This change in the revenue model can create win-win situations for universities and enterprises alike.

Translating Academic Approaches to Enterprise Learning

Designing effective skills-education programs for enterprise learners requires a distinctly different approach compared to the design of traditional academic programs. Within higher education, individual faculty members are generally the gatekeepers of knowledge for students. Student outcomes are taken into account during the initial phases of course design, but academic coursework is, first and foremost, a vehicle for knowledge acquisition (learning new facts and concepts). Accordingly, future iteration tends to focus solely on refining structure and content. Enterprise learning places a greater emphasis on skill acquisition (learning to perform a task or activity) and produces developments focused on improving applicability and outcomes. Designing a training program for an enterprise team requires a nuanced approach with a keen understanding of the learner's goals, constraints, and overall work context. Faculty are often ill-equipped to design training programs that align with the skills education needs of specific audiences of working learners.

Because of this disconnect, universities must seek out an intermediary to translate faculty knowledge into practical training for an enterprise client: the learning and development expert. Learning and development experts can lead the design and implementation of high-impact enterprise learning programs, working collaboratively with enterprise partners and faculty experts throughout the process.

A healthy tension may exist at times in the university-enterprise partnership. Given that the faculty approach to course design is often fundamentally different from an enterprise learning approach, L&D must work from the beginning to establish mutual respect for the knowledge on both sides of the partnership. A critical balance between advancing thought leadership and acknowledging existing corporate processes is required. This dynamic can strengthen the overall design process, leading to new understandings of how best to present and utilize learning materials.

Universities committed to developing enterprise learning programs should actively work to recruit and retain their own learning and development experts. As noted previously, it's typical for L&D experts to design and lead a program in the enterprise learning market. These experts will retain a vital role in the university-enterprise partnership. Learning and development experts focus on understanding the learner, the needs of the enterprise, and the training outcomes. By exploring these areas for some time during the design phase, L&D experts can arrive at a product that engages and prepares the learner.

These experts start with the broader corporate need to understand enterprise learners and their development process. They are uniquely suited to bridge faculty knowledge and corporate need, identifying how best to marry the two. L&D becomes the Rosetta Stone, a translation tool between relevant knowledge and current learning needs. An L&D expert necessarily plays the role of helpful go-between and interpreter at each stage of the process.

With a clear understanding of the learning needs, expected outcomes, and enterprise environment, the L&D experts will also be well-positioned to determine which training components could reside online and which would benefit from an in-person experience.

Case Study: ASU CareerCatalyst

Arizona State University's CareerCatalyst program provides a framework for implementing a learner-centric design approach in an enterprise setting.

Arizona State University (ASU) CareerCatalyst is part of the university's Learning Enterprise. The Learning Enterprise, launched as one of three "pillars" of ASU in 2019, exists to foster and grow universal access to social and economic opportunities at every stage of a person's life. To do so, the Learning Enterprise team advances this vision by building ecosystems for outcomes-driven lifelong learning. They lead and facilitate work with ASU's schools and colleges to develop scalable, technology-enabled offerings that serve non-degree learners throughout their lifetimes, from pre-K to post-retirement.

Within ASU's Learning Enterprise, CareerCatalyst represents the university-wide portfolio for non-degree career education, which includes programs and innovations in enterprise learning. As discussed, thriving in today's increasingly dynamic workplace requires working people to continue learning and acquiring new skills at every stage of their careers.

ASU, as the top-tier university for innovation, has incredible resources to provide broad career education to meet the rapidly evolving workforce's needs. The vision of CareerCatalyst is to leverage ASU resources—including expertise from over 800 academic programs and majors, ASU's physical infrastructure, and more—to build and scale an integrated portfolio of career education assets that serve learners at every career stage and provides employers with a skilled workforce.

Employer success depends on a workforce prepared to use a wide range of skills. To serve this need, CareerCatalyst has a broad approach to skills education. Learners need skills from two major domains. First, they need human skills, such as those related to communication and collaboration, which are relevant across functional roles and, due to their interpersonal nature, are unlikely to be automated. Second, learners need technical or functional skills which are more industry or role-specific. Technical skills can relate to virtually any discipline, from engineering to finance to teaching. The CareerCatalyst approach aligns all these skill types with the learning needs of individuals at the entry, middle, advanced, and executive skill levels.

Figure 12.1 ASU CareerCatalyst Framework for Skill Building

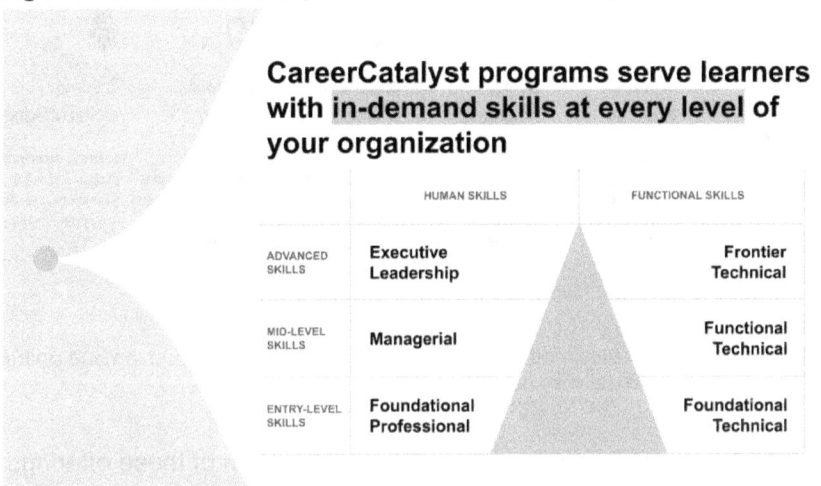

Note. The figure represents the two dimensions and three skill levels that CareerCatalyst uses to identify all possible enterprise learning audiences.

CareerCatalyst programs leverage ASU's expertise in partnership with internal L&D experts to provide skills education to learners at every level and talent transformation programs for employers. CareerCatalyst programs come in various modalities, from in-person programs in a classroom or a lab to entirely online, on-demand, or synchronous programs. The goal is to align the delivery modality to the needs and goals of learners and, in the case of enterprise training, to the needs and goals of their employers as well.

Figure 12.2 Spectrum of CareerCatalyst Learning Modalities

IN-PERSON		HYBRID	ONLINE		
Custom in-person programs	**In-person offerings**	**Hybrid programs**	**Self-paced offerings**	**Live online learning**	**Tailored digital offerings**
High-touchpoint, leading-edge, face-to-face custom delivery	High-touch, leading-edge, face-to-face delivery with open attendance	Combines leading-edge, face-to-face delivery and scalability of digital delivery	250+ continuing and professional education courses	Synchronous programs for cohorts of learners to engage live with instructors and peers	Learning experience designed based on your specific needs, live or on-demand.

Note. The figure showcases modality offerings on a spectrum of in-person and online modalities, with hybrid delivery noted in between.

Hybrid designs involve implementing a spectrum of these offerings. CareerCatalyst views hybrid learning in terms of both delivery channels (e.g., remote, in-person) and learner experience (e.g., individual, collaborative, self-paced, instructor-led). Different delivery channels, the where can be combined with different learner experiences, the when and how. Different delivery channels and learning experiences can even be combined within courses—self-paced online material combined with instructor-led training, live online learning programs combined with tailored in-person capstones.

CareerCatalyst combines these dimensions to meet diverse learning needs and create multiple access points with lower barriers to entry across a range of learners' circumstances. Custom hybridization is a critical tool to take each learner group's needs into account during course design and development. In some cases, learners can choose how they approach a particular activity (i.e., either synchronously or asynchronously). Because this hybridization is not possible in learning built on a single channel or experience, an effective enterprise learning approach must, by definition, be hybrid.

In certain corporate partnerships, beginning with asynchronous learning allows "level-setting," wherein expectations and knowledge form a foundation for subsequent live training. Other corporate partners with CareerCatalyst have used hybrid learning as a chance to build productive learning cultures in their workplaces purposefully. This is accomplished through synchronous online training to spur leadership to think through their work from a new perspective.

In this approach, CareerCatalyst then proceeds to develop a general learning experience that applies to the partner's entire body of employees. Leaders benefit from newly discovered or rediscovered knowledge and purpose in their roles. They are now sufficiently prepared by previous rounds of training to develop a culture and follow up with employees to actively support successful learning transfer.

CareerCatalyst Design Overview

The ADDIE model associates five steps with successful instructional design: Analysis, Design, Development, Implementation, and Evaluation. Each step of this traditional approach adapts to CareerCatalyst's new design approach, which infuses the steps with the flagship principles of design thinking: user empathy and iterative implementation. The resulting process incorporates learner empathy and focuses on intentional design—emphasizing purpose over product.

Figure 12.3 CareerCatalyst Design Overview

User research →	Design →	Build →	Launch ◆
Using a variety of tools, explore and document the needs of people seeking the training.	With user data as the foundation, design a course experience that will emotionally engage, intellectually challenge, and practically prepare people for careers.	Working with internal and external teams, build learning experiences that match design aspirations and are accessible to all.	Bring the course to market with the support of university marketing capacities. Support the course and faculty throughout the experience.

Note. The figure demonstrates the carefully framed steps of the CareerCatalyst design process.

In this approach, the CareerCatalyst design team begins with **user research** that provides real-world data, testimonials, and additional context to clarify the learning goals. This research can also inform the application of design thinking principles and choice of hybrid modalities. Establishing the purpose of products early in the instructional design process gives a realistic estimate of what hybrid delivery and engagement can meet the learners' needs. This requisite ensures we are analyzing potential learners' needs and shaping designs empathetic to those needs.

In some cases, learning designers will focus mostly on workplace skills needs and the gap between current and desired future capabilities. This is an important step that ensures employees can meet the needs of the business. However, this often leaves employees' needs and drivers out of the training development process. For this reason, each course development effort begins with several rounds of learner-focused analysis, understanding end users and the market's needs through research. This research provides a foundation to build learning experiences that exceed learners' expectations and empower them to apply their new skills immediately.

CareerCatalyst tailors modifications and enhancements to target particular audiences based on initial learner research and enterprise needs. This research also allows the team to determine the optimal learning modality for a course and how different hybrid options might best serve the customer. Two key questions the CareerCatalyst team often looks at when considering hybrid options are:

1. **Which models of hybrid work is the customer currently using?** The phrase "hybrid work" covers a broad range of implementations. Understanding an enterprise customer's existing approaches to hybrid and enabling technologies can provide insights into the format and topics of the training.
2. **How can we leverage enabling technologies with which employees are familiar?** Too often, training is limited to a single platform, usually an LMS. However, enterprise technologies such as Slack can be used to reinforce training and provide reminders to employees. Often employers don't think of these tools as "training platforms." Still, many have robust content delivery capabilities and can track elements such as reads and allow for reactions, threaded discussions, and more.

Upon moving to the *design* phase, the team internalizes the inputs from the research phase: We focus on an experience that meets learners where they are—exhibiting empathy for their circumstances and needs. This includes whether learners need specific levels of engagement during the process, whether they require in-depth skill and knowledge checks, and even what kind of environment will help them retain and transfer their learning. CareerCatalyst considers the needs analysis from the user research stage, among other insights, to learn what engages and motivates these learners. Incorporating these elements of engagement and motivation comes from the use of *emotional design* while calibrating the breadth, depth, intellectual challenge, and rigor of the course to an appropriate level—and of course, the hybrid modalities that suit this design brief.

Emotional design often refers to the presentation of learning material, with "emotion" frequently translating to the strategic use of color and anthropomorphic features. [6] While keeping this in mind, the CareerCatalyst team also uses tools like instructional storytelling to create initial and sustained engagement in a course as well as scenarios and other instructional techniques to personalize learning material. Doing so helps to improve learner engagement and learning transfer to the workplace—the ultimate purpose of the product. Design thinking approaches call for this mindfulness of purpose; meanwhile, learner empathy gives CareerCatalyst products a unique ability to deliver on that purpose.

In considering these design decisions, the team does not focus on implementing any specific modality—in-person, online, synchronous, or asynchronous. Instead, CareerCatalyst always uses these components to meet the respective needs of the chosen design approach. In the previous example, the corporate partner required assistance laying the groundwork for top-down support of their training initiatives. This support included developing a productive transfer climate. As a result of the chosen design, the organization's leaders use synchronous training to cooperate, communicate, and collaboratively learn the importance of the work and subject matter. This preceding training equips them to act as subject matter experts and guides for the more general asynchronous learning assigned to all employees. This hybrid approach lays the groundwork for a top-down approach to incorporate training into long-term outcomes. It even creates an environment that increases the value placed upon learned information as a cornerstone of newly built or adapted processes.

As the CareerCatalyst team **builds** the courses, faculty involvement becomes the source of learning material. With design thinking principles in mind, the team looks at the intended purpose of the course and decide

---

[6] Academic research into emotional design has often used the addition of human figures to illustrations to increase "relatability."

together with faculty what material best addresses that purpose. However, nothing produced remains forever tied to a specific deliverable. CareerCatalyst can move forward with an outline, recorded interviews, or other output from SMEs. The team can then turn this output into fuel for instructional storytelling, podcasts, written content, in-person lectures, activities, video lectures, and more. The medium of delivery is catered across hybrid modalities to fit learners' needs. The team designs the experience from the ground up to meet a learner's needs and must do the same when it comes to building learning offerings.

Working with Faculty

Faculty members are rich sources of expertise and the primary subject matter experts for CareerCatalyst projects. However, in a research institution like ASU, faculty members play several roles: instructor, researcher, mentor, and advisor, to name just a few. Given the myriad demands on their time, the CareerCatalyst team must leverage faculty resources carefully during the design and build periods. The team plans extensively and progress purposefully to maximize their available time and create the greatest possible impact.

Specific methods for this approach differ by course, but each requires us to iteratively refine learning objectives with the faculty member to leverage their unique knowledge, perspective, and existing assets (e.g., existing course material that could be repurposed for an enterprise audience). We seat the faculty intentionally (and rightly) in the role of SME throughout the design phase. Design processes range from full-sentence outlines covering outcome-related questions to proposed course templates, including input on presentation, interaction, and assessment. Each of these deliverables will become the basis for elements within the course that help accomplish its learning outcomes.

Intentional emphasis is also placed on the practical nature of content that faculty outline or produce. This emphasis ensures that learners receive steps to applicable processes that demonstrate skill acquisition. Faculty, in essence, provide the recipe that leads to a learning outcome—everything from the resources or ingredients the learner needs to the steps they must follow.

When developing the Professional Skills for Everyone series, the team asked faculty to create detailed outlines and then built them out into user-friendly, learner-centric content with content developers. In the same vein, the Grow with Google Sustainability Analyst series involved in-depth interviews with subject matter experts that we then similarly expanded upon. In contrast, recent work on sustainability with a large corporate customer has been of sufficient technical complexity that faculty are directly involved with content creation. In this case, the CareerCatalyst team adjusted faculty compensation accordingly to recognize the increasing contribution.

Table 12.4 CareerCatalyst Faculty Deliverables

	For Everyone **Faculty Deliverables**
Full-Sentence Outlines	Outlines form the basis of all content. The following topics are required: • Provide a working definition of the course focus (e.g., sharing a working definition of creative thinking). • Outline the resources required to engage in a task. These resources may be tangible (markers and flipcharts) or intangible (knowledge of people who are attending a meeting). Assembling these resources may require input and explanation. • Describe how to use these resources in an explicit task. This explicit task is the skill the person will learn through the course.
Assessment Recommendations	Faculty provide a recommendation of an assessment for the primary skills taught. These should connect easily to a workplace-specific implementation of the skill. Faculty may recommend multiple assessment types, and the L&D experts will select one for use.
Video Shoots Based On Written Script	While not mandatory, faculty are welcome to participate in video shoots on their content. In cases where faculty are unavailable to participate, hired talent will shoot the video.

Note. The table lists and describes common faculty deliverables used in the CareerCatalyst design process.

Subject matter contributions in and of themselves do not necessitate a faculty member's role in the course design process. Their level of involvement with learning design experts will depend on a number of factors and always happen in collaboration with learning design experts. These respective experts will collaborate to discover what's needed for learners to successfully reach their objectives: the resources they need, options to carry out skill-based activities, and methods to determine the effectiveness of said activities.

Faculty members possess invaluable expertise in the areas most relevant to the training topic at hand. Similarly, CareerCatalyst maintains expertise in course design and development. The team also retains responsibility for guiding the implementation of the learning experience, having found that faculty are open to and excited about this aspect of working with CareerCatalyst—it frees them to be subject matter experts and learn from the CareerCatalyst team's expertise in course design and development. This also allows CareerCatalyst to ensure the consistency of learning experiences across different courses and product lines while attending to factors such as clarity and accessibility.

Looking to the Future in Hybrid Enterprise Learning

Considering the audience's needs is critical to consider in any learning and development approach. Learners will have specific goals that the course must help them accomplish. Enterprise learning, as one type of L&D vertical, requires specific learning outcomes: Namely, learners should acquire relevant, timely skills to equip them for the present and future job landscape. For enterprise learning to be effective in this current workforce, it must adopt hybrid design and delivery—catering to the demands of industries embracing hybrid work models. We must keep in mind the needs of learners and their enterprises—encouraging a learning design approach that focuses these needs into the desired outcome at every turn. Design thinking, learner empathy, and a versatile set of resources make hybrid enterprise learning the most significant catalyst for the careers of present and future professionals.

References

Charaba, C. (2022, June 28). *Employee retention: The real cost of losing an employee.* PeopleKeep. Retrieved January 12, 2023, from https://www.peoplekeep.com/blog/employee-retention-the-real-cost-of-losing-an-employee

Glint. *Employee Well-Being Report.* (2021, May 1). Retrieved October 31, 2022, from https://www.glintinc.com/wp-content/uploads/2021/05/Glint-May-2021-Employee-Well-Being-Report.pdf

Flynn, J. (2022, October 12). *20 Stunning Great Resignation Statistics [2022]: Why Are Americans Leaving Their Jobs? – Zippia.* Zippia. Retrieved November 14, 2022, from https://www.zippia.com/advice/great-resignation-statistics/

Grossman, R., & Salas, E. (2011, May 13). The transfer of training: what really matters. *International Journal of Training and Development, 15*(2), 103–120. Wiley Online Library. https://doi.org/10.1111/j.1468-2419.2011.00373.x

SHRM. *Interactive Chart: How Historic Has the Great Resignation Been?* (2022, March 9). https://www.shrm.org/resourcesandtools/hr-topics/talent-acquisition/pages/interactive-quits-level-by-year.aspx

Malik, S. (2020, December 7). *Skills Transformation For The 2021 Workplace.* IBM. Retrieved January 13, 2023, from https://www.ibm.com/blogs/ibm-training/skills-transformation-2021-workplace/

Nunes, A. (2021, November 2). *Automation Doesn't Just Create or Destroy Jobs — It Transforms Them.* Harvard Business Review. Retrieved November 15, 2022, from https://hbr.org/2021/11/automation-doesnt-just-create-or-destroy-jobs-it-transforms-them

Reuveni, B. (2021, August 25). *Career development isn't linear and how to keep up*. Fast Company. Retrieved January 15, 2023, from https://www.fastcompany.com/90668481/careers-are-no-longer-ladders-to-climb-heres-how-to-develop-professionally-instead

Tonhäuser, C., & Büker, L. (2016). Determinants of Transfer of Training: A Comprehensive Literature Review. *International Journal for Research in Vocational Education and Training*, 3(2), 127–165. Hamburg State and University Library. https://doi.org/10.13152/IJRVET.3.2.4

LinkedIn. *2022 Workplace Learning Report: The Transformation of L&D*. (n.d.). The Transformation of L&D (p. 31). Retrieved November 15, 2022, from https://learning.linkedin.com/content/dam/me/learning/en-us/pdfs/workplace-learning-report/LinkedIn-Learning_Workplace-Learning-Report-2022-EN.pdf

PwC. *Upskilling Hopes and Fears 2021*. (n.d.). Retrieved December 15, 2022, from https://www.pwc.com/gx/en/issues/upskilling/hopes-and-fears.html

LinkedIn. *Where Internal Mobility Is Most Common Since COVID-19: Top Countries, Industries, and Jobs*. (2020, October 28). Retrieved October 31, 2022, from https://www.linkedin.com/business/talent/blog/talent-strategy/where-internal-mobility-is-most-common

Wigert, B., & Pendell, R. (2022, March 15). *The Future of Hybrid Work: 5 Key Questions Answered With Data*. Gallup. Retrieved November 15, 2022, from https://www.gallup.com/workplace/390632/future-hybrid-work-key-questions-answered-data.aspx

Afterword

The AI Revolution in Hybrid College Education

Kimberly Merritt, Elizabeth P. Callaghan, Stephen M. Kosslyn

Abstract

Artificial Intelligence (AI) is poised to revolutionize hybrid college education, which is a blend of traditional face-to-face and distance-learning instruction with online learning components (both synchronous and asynchronous). AI will offer new opportunities for personalization, efficiency, and accessibility. This chapter delves into the various ways that AI is set to affect hybrid college education and the potential challenges and implications that may arise.

Personalized Learning

One of the most significant benefits of generative AI (hereafter referred to just as "AI") in hybrid college education is the ability to provide personalized learning experiences. AI can do this by customizing both online and synchronous components of hybrid classes. AIs can analyze student data—such as learning preferences, strengths, and weaknesses—to create tailored learning pathways. The integration of AI in the asynchronous online components of hybrid learning allows course content and delivery to be adjusted in real-time, providing a more engaging and effective learning experience. AI can also play a role in synchronous components, both online (e.g., via Zoom) and in person. It can act as a tutor and guide that is always present, ready, and willing to interact with students (even to the extent of playing specific roles in active learning role-playing games).

Because AIs sometimes "hallucinate" information, answering incorrectly or making things up, it's best to provide source materials (such as relevant articles and chapters) and instruct the AI to base all responses only on those resources. This practice greatly reduces the problem, but it may not entirely eliminate it. Thus, the instructor must check all "prompts" (i.e., instructions and requests) to an AI, and ensure that the results are as expected.

Enhanced Student Support

AI-powered chatbots and virtual teaching assistants can provide round-the-clock support to students, answering queries, offering feedback, and guiding them through coursework. This increased support can reduce the burden on instructors and provide students with immediate assistance when they need it. Additionally, AI can help identify struggling students and provide targeted interventions, ensuring they receive much of the necessary support to succeed in their studies. However, AIs are not a substitute or replacement for humans, and must be monitored by a qualified person. One advantage of AIs is that they are always on and always accessible, so with the proper management and prompting from experts, AIs can provide timely feedback.

Efficient Content Creation and Assessment

AI can also streamline the process of content creation for hybrid college courses, allowing educators to develop engaging and interactive course materials efficiently. For example, AI-driven content generation tools can assist in creating lectures, quizzes, and other learning resources—and can tailor them to students' individual needs. Furthermore, AI can revolutionize the assessment process by automating grading and providing detailed feedback on student performance. Although this feedback needs to be vetted by an instructor, initial feedback generation not only saves time and resources but also enables educators to focus on higher-order tasks, such as developing new course materials or engaging with students on a personal level.

Increased Access to Education

AI has the potential to greatly expand access to hybrid college education by reducing costs and offering flexible learning options. Online course materials powered by AI can be easily updated and scaled to reach more students, while AI-driven language translation tools can break down language barriers and create a more inclusive learning environment. Additionally, AI can help educational institutions develop more affordable and efficient systems, making hybrid college education more accessible to a broader audience.

Challenges and Ethical Considerations

Although AI holds immense promise for revolutionizing hybrid college education, it also presents unique challenges and ethical considerations. Privacy concerns may arise as AI systems collect and analyze vast amounts of student data to provide personalized learning experiences. Educational institutions must ensure that they have appropriate measures in place to protect student privacy and comply with data protection regulations. Moreover, addressing potential biases in AIs is crucial to prevent discrimination and ensure that all students receive an equitable education. Institutions must continuously monitor and refine their uses of AI systems to minimize any unintended biases and work towards creating more inclusive learning environments.

Conclusion

The integration of AI into hybrid college education has the potential to transform learning experiences, making them more personalized, efficient, and accessible. As AI continues to advance, educational institutions must carefully consider the potential challenges and ethical implications while harnessing the power of AI to enhance the quality and reach of hybrid college education. With thoughtful implementation, AI can serve as a powerful tool in shaping the future of hybrid learning and in fostering an inclusive and dynamic educational landscape.

www.ingramcontent.com/pod-product-compliance
Lightning Source LLC
Chambersburg PA
CBHW070616030426
42337CB00020B/3816